# Porridge with Honey

## Martyn Ludlow

PARTRIDGE

Copyright © 2021 by Martyn Ludlow.

| ISBN: | Hardcover | 978-1-5437-6340-9 |
| | Softcover | 978-1-5437-6341-6 |
| | eBook | 978-1-5437-6342-3 |

All rights reserved. No part of this book may be used or reproduced by any means, graphic, electronic, or mechanical, including photocopying, recording, taping or by any information storage retrieval system without the written permission of the author except in the case of brief quotations embodied in critical articles and reviews.

Because of the dynamic nature of the Internet, any web addresses or links contained in this book may have changed since publication and may no longer be valid. The views expressed in this work are solely those of the author and do not necessarily reflect the views of the publisher, and the publisher hereby disclaims any responsibility for them.

Print information available on the last page.

**To order additional copies of this book, contact**
Toll Free +65 3165 7531 (Singapore)
Toll Free +60 3 3099 4412 (Malaysia)
orders.singapore@partridgepublishing.com

www.partridgepublishing.com/singapore

# Contents

About the Author ................................................................ vii
Foreword ................................................................................ ix
Dedication .......................................................................... xiii
Introduction ..................................................................... xxiii

1. Let's Get Started ............................................................. 1
2. Can You See Your Dreams Yet? ................................... 6
    Vision ............................................................................ 12
3. What Are Your Targets? ................................................17
    Love your obstacles .................................................... 22
    Inspect what you expect ........................................... 26
4. How Will You React . . . To Everything? ................. 28
    Bonsai Trees ................................................................ 34
    Don't Be Afraid to Succeed ...................................... 36
    Monster Me ................................................................. 41
    Do You Believe . . . In You? ..................................... 44
    Dealing with Grief ..................................................... 48
    Why Is It Important to Be Grateful? ...................... 49
    Clippety Clop, Clippety Clop ................................. 50
    Chitter Chatter, Chitter Chatter, Chit, Chit, Chit ........ 54
5. Habits ............................................................................. 56
6. Focus ...............................................................................74
7. Scared to Fail? Not Anymore! ..................................... 79
8. Why Now and Not Tomorrow ................................... 87
    Clutter .......................................................................... 89

| | |
|---|---|
| The Two Pains | 91 |
| Distraction | 92 |
| Don't-Do List | 92 |
| 9. Taking Action | 94 |
| The Ivy Lee Method | 103 |
| Efficient versus Effective | 106 |
| My Warrior Program | 107 |
| 10. Get Some Skin in the Game | 109 |
| 11. Keep the Confidence, Ditch the Ego | 112 |
| 12. Could You Change? | 115 |
| 13. Learning and Education | 118 |
| 14. Intelligence versus Wisdom: It's Your Call | 126 |
| 15. Family and Friends | 128 |
| 16. Happiness | 136 |
| 17. Relationships | 144 |
| 18. Why Travel and Who You Could Meet | 149 |
| 19. Health, Wealth, and Well-Being | 152 |
| Exercise | 156 |
| Wealth | 157 |
| Well-Being | 163 |
| Mental Health | 164 |
| 20. Giving Back | 168 |
| 21. This Is Tomorrow Calling | 171 |
| | |
| Suggested Further Reading | 183 |
| Thanks and Acknowledgements | 185 |

# About the Author

Martyn Ludlow was born in Merthyr Tydfil, South Wales, in 1959.

From a humble beginning, he has endured the rollercoaster of life, tasting many of life's pleasures and witnessing some dramatic personal failures.

He has built many small businesses and enjoyed a successful career in the corporate world, developing a love for coaching and mentoring. His love of personal development has resulted in the delivery of many speeches in many different countries.

He has a wicked, even naughty, sense of humor, which he uses to raise money for charity as a standup comedian.

Martyn has worked in many countries and now lives in Hong Kong.

He has two sons, whom he adores, and at the time of writing, three beautiful granddaughters, the inspiration for this book.

A keen student of personal development, he has learnt from the best and invested a lot of time and money to improve his performance and life.

Martyn is currently battling stage 4 cancer and receiving chemotherapy. It was during this treatment that he decided to write the book.

He wants to pass on some simple advice to his grandchildren and introduce them to great thinking from people who have inspired him.

Although aimed as a message to his grandchildren, this will be of interest to anyone wanting to improve themselves.

This is Martyn's first book. The second is well on its way.

*Porridge with Honey* is Martyn's legacy to his grandchildren.

# Foreword

On any sunny Sunday afternoon, the expat community of Mui Wo can reliably and mostly be found in the dockside pub, China Bear, the most popular watering hole on Rural Lantau Island.

As pubs go, it is nothing fancy, but it has three things going for it.

The service may be tardy, but it is friendly.

The location is perfect, with its waterside view of Silvermine Bay—Hong Kong skyline visible in the distance.

Then there is the clientele; for a local, there will always be a few friends in attendance, sometimes many.

After lunch, there is usually quite a hubbub; expats from all around the world provide an alphabet soup of languages and accents.

Today one accent cuts through the background chatter; distinctly, unusually, and unmistakably, it belongs to South Wales.

You do not hear it often.

Curiously, I turn to locate the owner; he is sitting at a table nearby with one of my American friends, Dave.

'Hey, Simon, come and join us, buddy. Meet Martyn Ludlow.'

Hong Kong expats inevitably introduce themselves with tales of where they came from and their life's journey: the journey that led them to Hong Kong usually. Martyn has just moved here from Hong Kong island.

A lively conversation ensues; Martyn is not introverted at all, and I am a good audience.

I quickly learn of his childhood in Merthyr Tydfil and all that came with that.

I am probably not typical amongst the audience of proximity because I have spent much time in Wales. I can see the places Martyn describes clearly in my mind.

In village life, one inevitably sacrifices a little privacy. The locals will introduce you in well-meaning ways, always appending some attribute that seems to sum you up in as few words as possible.

In my case, I have written a book, and inevitably, this comes up.

This particular evening is no different, and the conversation is headed down that path. Martyn and I talk about writing, how it is similar to talking about that which you most care about, but much more important, because talk is transitory, writing is not.

Martyn explains his life to me in an unguarded way and confides that as a relatively recent grandparent, he yearns to create an enduring message for his three granddaughters: Skylah, Chanel, and Tienna; a simple memoir and some advice the girls will value as they grow up. He told me that he has been thinking of this for some time.

I ran into Martyn a few days later, and he announces that he has begun to write.

Many months have passed, and Martyn has done much more than that. He has written *Porridge with Honey*.

*Porridge with Honey* is a charming, heartfelt message for the future and some good advice that we all can use.

Simon McCartney, Author of *The Bond*
Mui Wo
January 2021

# Dedication

It is easier writing to you as a granddad, having been blessed with wonderful grandparents myself and the special influence they had on my life. They gave me experiences I still visit when I need them and a grounding that could never be bought. I want to share some of my experiences with you.

At thirteen years old, Nanny was a parent of five siblings. Her mum died, leaving her in charge, without an instruction manual. There was no time for her childhood or school. She assumed an enormous amount of responsibility and did her job so well that her siblings all died before her. Imagine that? You dedicate your life to your family, and you outlive them all.

Nanny controlled the money and just about everything else (including Willy).

Every Friday, after work, Willy would tip up his pay packet to her, and she would give him his pocket money for the week, 30 bob (shillings) or £1.50 in today's terms. This was before decimalised currency. She deserves a book herself.

She didn't work. She couldn't. Nanny was the queen of our castle, and we all knew it. Although she ran the family with an iron fist, when it came to her grandchildren, it always found a soft landing, thankfully, as she was a big lady in every way, in stature, heart, and generosity. She would never have money, it all went on us, and Willy didn't dare ask.

She's a hostess like no other, everyone wanted to visit, and they did, very often and without notice. Nanny and Willy lived in a small terraced house, and I still cannot understand how so many people stayed with us. Where did we put them? This is a big family, but we did. I loved it, growing up with a close family, the smells from the kitchen, the noise from Willy's tool shed, and the wonderful conversations by the fireside.

Their address was at 105 Gilfach Cynon, Twynyrodyn, a small terraced house—two up, two down with a DIY extension for a kitchen and bathroom—they bought about one hundred years ago, and they lived there until they died. Yes, Willy built this himself. There was no planning permission then, or this would not have happened. The roof was corrugated zinc sheets resting on uneven breeze blocks, but the coal fire kept us warm in the winter. He was a miner, and coal was free.

Here's to Nanny . . .

### A Grandmother Just Like You

*I just wanted to let you know*
*You mean the world to me*
*Only a heart as dear as yours*
*Would give so unselfishly*
*The many things you've done*
*All the times that you were there*
*Help me know deep down inside*
*How much you really care*

*Even though I might not say*
*I appreciate all you do*
*Richly blessed is how I feel*
*Having a grandmother just like you*

My grandfather was so lovable, especially after a few beers. He would sing (awfully). I still cringe when I think of him singing the 'Rose of Tralee.' That was for Nanny. Her name was Mary, and she was his rose. Nanny had Irish roots, of which she was proud. I would love to hear it again.

One night—1965, I think—he came home early from the Merthyr Labour Club. We were up late. It was Christmas. We were allowed. We called him Grampa, with affection. It was that night that he said, 'Don't call me Grampa, it makes me feel old, call me Willy,' and from then on, everyone called him Willy.

A simple humble man without a formal education beyond fourteen years old, a quiet, calm demeanour hid his huge integrity. He could be trusted with anything. A real grafter who went straight down the coal mine at fourteen and stayed in that job until he retired, he spent two periods of more than a year in hospital when the pit caved in on him. He went back to work as soon as he come out of hospital.

He kept his metal sandwich box well into retirement, which had tales of the rats he shared his sandwiches with underground, and there was nowhere to wash his hands. Hard men, hard times.

The accidents didn't kill him, but the pit did. He eventually died of pneumonoconiosis—coal dust on the chest.

We would spend hours walking in Glemile Woods, and he would educate me.

The woods were close to our home, about a twenty-minute walk. We swam in the pond, made a swing from the high trees that took us over the pond, camped, cooked, and laughed. Oh, the stories around the campfire. We laid night lines to catch fish for breakfast. So many bones in Perch, but it tasted like an adventure on a plate, a dirty plate. We looked after one another.

There was no trouble in the woods, the bad guys didn't go there, and Twyn had its share of bad guys. It was us and nature. 'What's that, Willy?' I would ask.

'It's a stoat,' he'd reply.

'What's a stoat, Willy?' I asked.

'It's like a polecat,' Willy replied.

'What's a polecat, Willy?

My education was beginning in a way that I could never buy. I got closer to nature and learnt to fix anything. (I wasn't so good at the latter though.)

Curiosity didn't kill this cat, and my curiosity was encouraged to grow with the patience I needed, and they needed patience with me.

Being the eldest son of three from a single-parent family, it helped my mother for me to live periodically with Nanny and Willy. That was no hardship for me.

We spent hours around that kitchen fire listening to great stories. The older Welsh people had great stories and learnt how to tell them well. Nanny would tell ghost stories, and the hairs at the back of my neck would stick up. Yes, the yarns were embellished a little. The Welsh are great orators.

They didn't have the distractions we have of the Internet and even TV. TV came later thankfully, as it didn't interfere with the stories (and there were only two channels then). So the stories had the glories.

We didn't use the bathroom either. I cannot remember if it ever had running water. It soon became a pigeon coop, and anyway, we were used to the tin bath by the fireplace. I forgot how many kettles of water Nanny had to boil to get enough hot water in the bath for us to be warm.

The backyard was Willy's sanctuary. His tool shed held equal rank to his pigeon coop. Our toilet nestled between them, about 20 metres further on. Yes, the toilet was outside. Not nice in the winter, so we used a bucket.

When he retired in 1965 (I think?), he started selling firewood to local pensioners. It was beer money for him but hard work.

He made a wheelbarrow from old wood resting on pram (stroller), wheels which he found at the rubbish tip. He was good at making things from other people's junk. This barrow looked like a coffin on wheels, but he could stack six large potato sacks of firewood on this thing and balance them all the way to his customers.

I could be involved at every stage of his little business empire. The wood came from railway sleepers. The railroads were diminishing then and disused. There were enough sleepers to keep him in business for his lifetime. They were soaked in oil from the trains, so great for burning, not sure about the health aspects though.

The sleepers would meet the modern technology of Willy's saw.

He rigged up a circular saw using a motor from a washing machine (also from the tip). No safety guard. Extension cables from the makeshift kitchen, which had extension cables from the house. I can still smell the sawdust and see him with his goggles on sawing the blocks. The neighbours didn't like the noise, but some of them were customers.

His saw cut the sleepers into blocks, and the rest was done by hand, his axe.

The potato bags were collected from the local grocery store, and his customers would save them for him after use. Mrs Jones from Wheatley Place was the best. She could use one bag five or six times. This was early recycling.

Outside the backyard was the Incky, a field that separated the terraced houses and the council houses. Everything happened on the Incky—sports, fighting, and fun; a real community. Its real name was the Incline, which got abbreviated over time.

I would cross the Incky to take a shortcut through our friends' gardens to my mother's house. The neighbours didn't mind. We had a path through two streets.

Trade happened on the Incky. Mrs Parry sold the best toffee apples ever and anything could be bought.

Bonfire night was a big occasion. There's a competition to get the biggest bonfire. We collected tyres, mattresses, and anything that would burn for weeks before.

We would even raid others' bonfires to make ours bigger, but don't tell Nanny and Willy. They wouldn't like that.

Here's to Willy . . .

### My Granddad

*My granddad kept a garden.*
*A garden of the heart;*
*He planted all the good things,*
*That gave our lives their start.*
*He turned us to the sunshine,*
*And encouraged us to dream:*
*Fostering and nurturing*
*The seeds of self-esteem.*
*And when the winds and rain came,*
*He protected us enough;*
*But not too much because he knew*
*We would stand up strong and tough.*
*His constant good example,*
*Always taught us right from wrong;*
*Markers for our pathway*
*That will last a lifetime long.*

Nanny and Willy would take us to the Donkey Derby at Mountain Hare, local guys riding wild ponies like the rodeo. I never did that. Willy wouldn't let me, so I would win the goldfish at the fair throwing Ping-Pong balls into glass bowls.

A wonderful community right outside my grandparents' back door.

Nanny and Willy fought like cat and dog. It was a different love that taught me so much—different but real. They could criticise each other, but no one else could, or you would face their wrath. I know, I saw many on the receiving end of that.

Together they influenced my life and decisions in many ways. They were a brake on me when I needed to slow down, and they often used those brakes to my enormous benefit.

They kept me out of trouble and supported me in everything.

The greatest gift they gave me was time, their time, time which shaped a great life for me.

Without knowing, they, together with my mother, gave me the roots to grow, the wings to fly, and it really felt like they were the wind beneath my wings.

They can't leave me because their blood still flows through my veins, like mine flows through yours. I inherited a pedigree that I am proud to pass on.

Their will and spirit still live in me. That's the spirit I am riding for this book.

As a very grateful grandson, I thank them for nurturing in me a confidence mixed with humility and a genuine love of my family and life.

I hope, in part, that I can wear their boots for this message to you, as I know I cannot fill them.

Thank you, Nanny and Willy, for the rules, values, and responsibilities you entrusted me with.

As a grateful grandson, I dedicate this book to my grandparents, Nanny and Willy.

# Introduction

I have two simple reasons for writing this book:

1. *I would love to be part of the inspiration* that helps motivate you to great achievements, avoid some mistakes, and live a happy life.
2. *I want to live forever.* What better way than to leave you with a book? This is my legacy to you.

I troubled with whether to address you as children or adolescents. I chose the latter to give this a longer lifespan and, hopefully, be of relevance to you at any age.

So this is your book, and in your book, you will be introduced to many great people throughout history who have shaped this world. They are on our team now through their legacy. Please seek them out throughout your life when you need them. They and their work are waiting to be discovered by you. As an immigrant, I bring them from all over the world. They are your team now.

For effect, I include poems, quotations, questions, stories, granddad tips, and some giggle juice.

All part of our language, knowledge, and inspiration. Where possible, I credit this team, but after many years, there will be some quotes that have inspired me, and I don't now know who the author is.

I've experienced stock market booms and crashes, same with property. I have known such wonderful love and experienced some horrible hate. I bring experience from all our wonderful continents and from many different cultures.

This is not a love story, but it is a story of love, a grandparent's love, which I hope you will one day experience and cherish. Then you will understand 'that there is no app to replace a lap.'

To be in your memories tomorrow, your book will help me be in your life today. This is a little dip into many important areas of your life. I doubt if much will have changed. Dip in and out whenever you want to. It's a light read, and hopefully, you can take a few snippets of value and make them yours.

Please read this at different times in your life. Your book won't change, but you will. It will have different meaning when you are a different person.

Nature gave us the rules. I'm just one shortcut to picking up the pebbles on your way.

(The pebbles are coming soon.)

I have been lucky enough to have visited every continent on earth. I have worked in Spain,

the UAE, France, and Asia. This exposure to different cultures has helped build me.

I have learnt that 'sometimes you find yourself in the middle of nowhere, and sometimes in the middle of nowhere, you find yourself.'

I have met many great coaches and inspirational figures, and I want to share some of this with you.

I've been guilty of some of the things I will ask you not to do and a beneficiary of the successful things I want to share. Please learn from me and the greats that inspired and helped me on my way, hopefully avoiding some of the mistakes I made on the way.

It will be many years before you realise what a force you are in my life. You filled a space I didn't know was empty.

A grandparent's love is different—not better, not worse, but different. Many say that one difference is that you can give the grandchildren back when you are finished with them.

Never once did I want to give you back. You were the best medicine when I was sick and a great source of fun and energy every time we were together.

At the time of writing, I live in Hong Kong. You blessed me with the name Gandad Honky Konky, a name I cherish.

So let the porridge be the soup that warms the cockles of your heart, and let the honey be the sweetness in your life and all the little pleasures.

There's so much I want to tell you and would love to make this perfect, but if I wait for perfection, this will never be printed. So here's my best shot at my imperfect best.

*A grandchild is a blessing*
*A gift from above*
*A precious little angel*
*To cherish and love*
*A wee bit of heaven*
*Drifted down from above*
*A handful of happiness*
*A heart full of love*

Come on, let's go, it's time to turn pages, create some memories, and let some granddad experience loose on you.

# 1

## Let's Get Started

Once upon a time, a long time ago, far, far away, there were three little children.

One day they wanted to plan a big adventure, and they decided to go into the scary forest. They knew they had to be careful as this forest had wolves, snakes, spiders, and many other dangers.

They carefully planned their adventure and packed some warm clothes, made jam sandwiches, and took bottles of water.

One of them had a special collection of pebbles, which she painted in bright colours. She loved the pebbles and took them everywhere.

They didn't tell Mummy and Daddy as they knew Mummy and Daddy would not want them to go into the scary forest alone.

So off they went, holding hands, skipping and laughing all the way. They were having so much fun that they didn't realise how far they had gone.

They liked being scared.

The trees were thick now, and it was getting dark.

They liked their big adventure, but it was starting to get scary.

'Too wit too woooooo,' whistled the owl.

'Howwwl,' cried the wolf.

'Hissssss,' slithered the snake.

It was time to go home.

When they turned around, there were many trees and many paths. 'How do we get home?' they thought. 'Which is the best path? Which direction do we take?'

Two of them thought of splitting up, but they thought, no, we must stick together to be safe.

They had eaten all their food and decided to make their way as quickly as possible as Mummy and Daddy would be worried, but they were lost in a scary forest and didn't know which path to take.

Until the sister with the pebbles said, 'Don't worry, I can get us home.'

'How can you do that?' the other two sisters asked.

She replied, 'Mummy and Daddy told me that if I worked hard and committed to something I love, that it would serve me in my future. I loved collecting and painting my pebbles, and on the way to this adventure, I dropped pebbles every few metres, so now all we have to do is follow the pebbles and we will be home safe.'

So they followed those pebbles and made their way home with a great lesson in life. They learnt the importance of commitment and hard work. It took many hours collecting and painting those pebbles. It took thought and skill to figure out how to use them, other than just to look pretty.

Your life will take you on a great adventure. I am leaving lots of pebbles, like stepping stones, to help you find *your* way to *your* destination.

It's your book, and I want it to ooze positivity.

Someone once said, 'To succeed in life, you need a wishbone, a backbone, and a funny bone.' These will come in handy for the pages ahead.

Are you ready for your adventure? If so, let's see what emotional gems we pick up on the way. We can do this together with our team of greats. Come on, open the door, and let your future in. We're off to look for pebbles because now we know their value and how to use them.

### 'Advice for My Granddaughter'

Robert A Hall
The world will break your heart, my girl,
Embrace it anyway.
You were a gift from God to us,
To turn despair away.
Enjoy each day you live, my girl,
For joy was made for you.
We see it in your happy smile,
And everything you do.

Now live a life of honour, girl,
Of hope and faith and trust.
For duty's just a word for love,
And doing what you must.
Now live for something great, my girl,
For something more than self.
True happiness in service lies,
That is the only wealth.
Now live a life of learning, girl,
And read a book a week.
For knowledge is the Holy Grail,
You'll never cease to seek.
Now be a friend of truth, my girl,
And judge folk by their deeds.
For empty words are honeyed traps,
And lies are evil's seeds.
Don't live to make us proud, my girl,
But live so you are proud.
Of everything you do in life,
And shun the evil crowd.
If reputation's lost, my girl,
Then life is but regrets.
So make your word your bond, my girl,
And always pay your debts.
If God is good to you, my girl,
And children come your way.
Don't pass support to someone else,
But parent every day.
Don't live for just today, my girl,
Or you will soon be bored.
The things in life worth having are
The things you work toward.

We do not wish you riches, girl,
By greed are many wrecked.
Contentment only comes to those
Who live with self-respect.
We do not wish you ease, my girl,
Existence free of strife.
But all the joy that's found within
*The purpose driven life.*

*A journey of a thousand miles starts with a single step.*
—Buddha

Now it's time to dream. Ready? Let's bring in the big guns.

# 2

# Can You See Your Dreams Yet?

*Children with dreams become leaders with vision.*

\*\*\*

*'To live, to love, to leave a legacy.'*

Let's start with the fun. The bit that gets your juices flowing, we will pick up the challenges on the way and deal with them. Why start here? Because you owe yourself the life you have always dreamt of.

Now imagine if you couldn't fail? What would you take on? Dealing with failure is later, but for now, it's dream time.

It starts with a dream—your dream. Let's go to the part of your brain that makes the dreams.

If something you loved was free, how much would you take? Dreaming is free, so why not gorge on it? Dreaming combined with vision is where the magic grows. Let's create some magic.

It's your dream.

When you are working on something you really care about, you don't have to be pushed.

Your vision pulls you there. Lighten the load, and enjoy the journey. It's a very exciting ride.

Do you wonder what's in store for you? What your future holds? Do you wonder where you are taking this? And why?

You can't change the world, but you can change *your* world, and it starts with *your* dreams.

The river of success will meander throughout your life. Doesn't matter where you jump in,

but you must jump in. Wherever you land, it will be different water. But don't just go with the flow. That's for dead fish. Swim against the tide. Sail that river with you in control. The river will take you, and it gets refreshed every day with new energy so long as it keeps moving. This is your momentum. Keep moving.

In the classic movie *Field of Dreams*, there's a great quote: 'If you build it, they will come.'

That's vision and belief, and that could apply to anything in your life.

One of the great dreamers of the last century was undoubtedly Walt Disney. His dreams and visions created memories for almost everyone on the planet. At the opening of the new Epcot Center in Florida, someone asked the CEO of Disney, long after Walt's death, what he thought Walt Disney would have thought had he seen this? The reply was 'Walt saw this—

many times.'

Walt Disney was also credited with saying, 'If you can dream it, you can do it.'

He and his movies provide us with many inspirational quotes. Here are samples:

> *First, think. Second, dream. Third, believe. And finally, dare.*
> —Walt Disney

> *All it takes is faith and trust.*
> —Peter Pan

> *Listen to your heart, you will understand.*
> —Grandmother Willow, *Pocahontas*

*Even miracles take a little time.*
—Fairy Godmother, *Cinderella*

*If you focus on what you left behind, you will never be able to see what lies ahead.*
—Gusteau, *Ratatouille*

*The flower that blooms in adversity is the most rare and beautiful of all.*
—The Emperor, *Mulan*

*Venture outside your comfort zone, the rewards are worth it.*
—Rapunzel

*Don't just fly, soar.*
—Dumbo

*Remember, you're the one who can fill the world with sunshine.*
—Snow White

*Now think of the happiest things, it's the same as having wings.*
—Peter Pan

*That was like a crazy trust exercise.*
—Anna, *Frozen*

*You don't have time to be timid. You must be bold and daring!*
—Lumiere, *Beauty and the Beast*

*There's the whole world at your feet.*
—Bert, *Mary Poppins*

*Open different doors, you may find a you there that you never knew was yours. Anything can happen.*
—Mary Poppins

*The moment you doubt whether you can fly, you cease forever to be able to do it.*
—Peter Pan

*I never look back, darling! It distracts me from now.*
—Edna Mode, *The Incredibles*

*I remember Daddy told me, 'Fairy tales can come true.' But you've got to make them happen, it all depends on you!*
—Tiana, *Princess and the Frog*

Napoleon Hill, in his bestselling book *Think and Grow Rich*, wrote, 'Whatever the mind can conceive and believe, it can achieve.' This is because we achieve in advance. We need to visualise and believe it first.

My hero of the '80s was Dr Denis Waitley. He has worked in the control rooms of NASA, coached Olympic athletes, and was one of the most sought-after keynote speakers. He asks the audience, 'What was the first thing Neil Armstrong said when he set foot on the moon?'

We all know now that he said so well, 'One small step for man, one giant leap for mankind.'

What did he say next? 'Just like drill, just like drill.'

They had practised so much, not even knowing the true conditions. No one had yet been to the moon. Yet they had visualised exactly what it would be like.

He says of winners that there never was a winner who didn't win in advance.

He tells us that our minds go through a process or pre-play and replay, and that's the vision we need.

If we get it right in drill, we will get it right in life.

Dreaming is free, and anyone can do it. And what are the side effects? In my experience, the side effects are lovely feelings and a confidence boost. What a way to live and start your day? So dream, dream big, and dream now. If this scares you, start small and watch it grow. Plant a dream seed. Look after it, and it will grow to look after you.

Although there are no bad side effects, there is a risk. Some will think you are crazy because they won't do it.

There is a magic in risking everything for a dream nobody sees but you, and when it comes true, it's one of the greatest feelings ever, and you can influence it. Shall we test it? Relax and clear your thoughts. Think about everything you want: relationships, money, health, education, travel, career, and spiritual. Now close your eyes and focus on these. Dream about them. Make it real. Include colour, sounds, smells, feelings. You have all these gifts. They want to work for you. This is not about finding yourself. It's about creating yourself.

Did you do it? If not, do it now. Please. Don't analyse it. Follow Nike's example and just do it.

How was it? We watch movies to get these feelings when, all along, we have them inside us, waiting to serve us. You can access them now.

**Granddad Tip: Trust yourself. If you don't believe, you won't make the effort.**

The biggest block to my dreams was my excuses. I got good at it. But here's the rub: I didn't realise for years that I was doing it. Watch this one: We are good at sometimes rationalising why not to do things. That's knocking on the door to failure.

Most people get up, go to work, come home, watch TV. Next day, get up, go to work, come home, watch TV. They do this for seventy-five years then die. This is a bad habit, and you were not created for this. So you can either hit the snooze button and go to sleep with your dreams or wake up and go and make them.

I don't think I need to show you how to dream, just to remind you to do it and do it often.

## Vision

*This is where you can be saved by your future.*

Find the soul in this. Please make this an obsession. Every winner I knew won in advance. They saw it first. They dreamt it. Just like Walt Disney and all the greats, if you can't see your riches in your vision, you will never see it in your bank balance.

One of the best musicians of the '70s was Stevie Wonder. His songs sold in their millions, and he is blind. He once said, 'Just because a man lacks the use of his eyes doesn't mean he lacks vision.' So we have no excuse.

There are world champions who, when they were infants, were in training: Tiger Woods, Bruce Lee, Lewis Hamilton, Kobe Bryant—the very best. They were not better than you are now. You can get in the top 10 of anything. This could be the beginning of everything you want.

I heard a lovely story once about the great Renaissance painter Michelangelo. In his day, he was the equivalent of a celebrity. One day he was hard at work, carving his famous sculpture *The Archangel Gabriel* when a class of school children arrived. They saw a large piece of marble and the artist chipping away at it with his tools.

A little girl asked, 'Why are you hitting that rock with your tools, sir?'

To which Michelangelo replied, 'Inside this rock is a beautiful angel. It's my job to set him free.'

Now that's vision at its best, and inside you is a beautiful angel. Let's set him or her free.

*Aim for the top. It's too crowded at the bottom.*

**Did you know?**

At the time of writing, some of the richest people alive are Jeff Bezos, founder of Amazon and the richest person alive in 2020; Warren Buffet, founder of Berkshire Hathaway and one of the richest people in the world; Reed Hastings, founder of Netflix; Michael Bloomberg, billionaire and former mayor of New York.

Guess what they did before they were a massive success? This surprised but inspired me.

Jeff Bezos was a cook at McDonald's.

Warren Buffet delivered newspapers as a teenager.

Reed Hastings sold vacuum cleaners door to door.

Michael Bloomberg worked at a car park.

They learnt to do what they could, with what they had, right where they were. No better than us but totally immersed in their dreams.

There will be some lumps and bumps on the way, but don't let life get in the way of your plans.

In ice hockey, a skater learns to look to where puck is going, not where it's been. He then skates towards the puck, knowing the puck isn't there yet. You are skating into a beautiful future that you haven't even created yet, but you know where it's going. We need to know where the puck is and where it has been, but that doesn't define us or determine where we're going. Your vision does that. Your action then defines or defeats you.

And to keep your dreams and vision in your face, consider a vision board.

**Vision Board**

I call mine Future Focus.

On a huge board or card in your private place, write down all your dreams and look at it every day. Use photos, clippings from magazines, colours, and quotations. If it's a car or home you want, get a photo or draw it.

This is great reminder of what you really want that you visit every day. Just wait until you feel the energy coming from your future. Fuel for your soul, creativity for today, and momentum now. What are you waiting for? Get started. Personalise it. Name it.

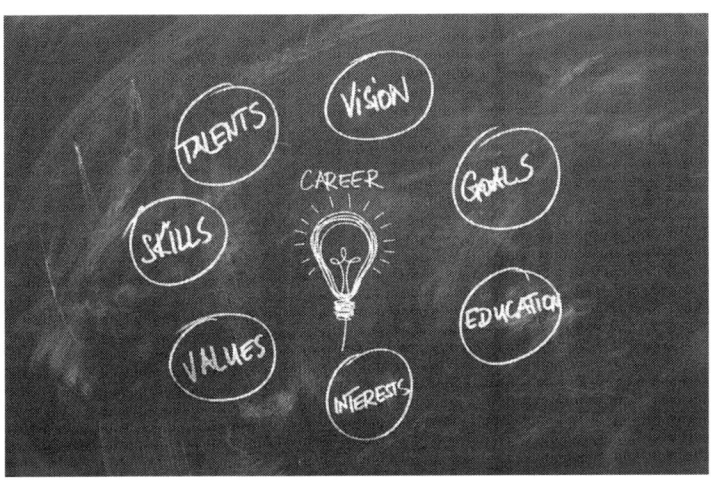

There is a part of your brain called the reticular activator that acts as a filter. If you focus on your vision every day, it will filter out a lot of the noise and stuff that is in your way. For example, TVs are on sale every day, but you do not see them, unless you are looking for a TV. They are still there but not on your radar. When you are looking, they all appear. Same with cars. You pass thousands every day without thinking about them, but when you want a yellow Volkswagen, they all appear. Same with your vision. If you focus on your vision every day, your brain will help steer you towards the resources and people you need to bring about your dreams.

Some further thoughts on vision from the greats:

*A man without a vision for his future always returns to his past.*
—Anonymous

*Microsoft was founded with a vision of a computer on every desk and in every home. We've never wavered from that vision.*
—Bill Gates

*If you want to turn a vision into reality, you have to give 100 percent and never stop believing in your dream.*
—Arnold Schwarzenegger

*Champions aren't made in the gyms. Champions are made from something they have deep inside them—a desire, a dream, a vision.*
—Muhammad Ali

*If you are working on something exciting that you really care about, you don't have to be pushed. The vision pulls you.*
—Steve Jobs

*Vision without execution is hallucination.*
—Thomas Edison

Don't have one foot in the past and one toe in the future. Dreams and vision are the seeds of greatness, so have the vision to build your dreams, or someone else will hire you to build theirs.

Dreaming and vision is where it starts . . . Now let the genie out of the bottle by rubbing her lamp with your goals.

# 3

# What Are Your Targets?

*A goal is a dream with a deadline.*

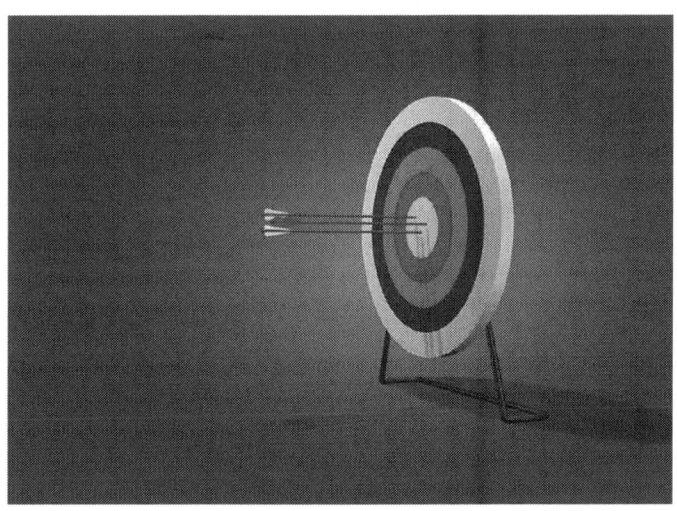

These are the stepping stones to your vision.

Don't waste a new year in an old mind. There's someone in hospital begging for your life. Get positively discontented. Now the goals. Let's go on a trip to the Goal Coast.

**Granddad Tip: We don't grow when everything is easy. We grow when we face challenges.**

*Why Goals?*

1. ***They guide your focus.***

To become someone different, you must do something different and focus on it. There's a power in working towards something you have decided to do. When it's written down and checked regularly, you are on the ball. We never run out of ideas. We run out of focus. Goals keep you on track.

2. ***They improve how you behave.***

When you are drawn to your goals you instill a better behaviour. This is your discipline. Nobody told you to do this. You decided, you planned, and you implemented. These are great behavioural attributes. Good behaviour leads to good habits and vice versa.

3. ***They get you going.***

Goals give us momentum. Achievement and progress are addictive. Athletes talk about being in the zone. They need achievement for that. Forward momentum gives us this. When you check off little achievements, you move on. This momentum creates good habits and vice versa.

4. ***They move you on to greater achievements.***

What do you do when you have accomplished a goal? You move on to a bigger and better goal. Look what's happening here? A series of achievements getting better every time.

5. ***They challenge you.***

Goals should play to your strengths and develop new capabilities. Write down everything you want or need to learn and make it a goal. Imagine if you achieved one new capability a month. Imagine if you had done that last year.

If you challenge yourself, get going, stay focussed, show great behaviour, and do it consistently, and then move on to greater achievements. What would that do for your life?

Goals in action really are dreams with deadlines. They should be out of reach but not out of sight. If they are not out of reach, they will not stretch you.

Set a goal so big so that you cannot achieve it until you grow into the person who can, and don't wait until you think you are good enough. Successful people never think they are good enough but keep getting better.

Get clear on the goals as these make up your vision and include an ambitious timescale. Elon Musk said, 'If you give yourself thirty days to clean your house, it will take thirty days. If you give yourself three hours, it will take three hours.' Same applies to your goals, ambition, and plans.

In the book *Alice in Wonderland*, there's a scene that follows: One day Alice came to a fork in the road and saw a Cheshire cat in a tree. 'Which road do I take?' she asked.

'Where do you want to go?' was his response.

'I don't know,' Alice answered.

'Then,' said the cat, 'it doesn't matter.'

*If you don't know where you are going, then any road will take you there.'*

**How do you set goals?**

**Granddad Tip: Before you start, get clarity on this. Clear your mind and focus. This is too important to rush with a cluttered head.**

1. **Write them down.**

Putting pen to paper creates a connection with your brain that's personal. It's your unique handwriting. Write down your goals and think carefully about the steps involved to get there. Writing something down improves recall, and having a physical reminder of what you want to achieve means you can check in and review it at any time.

2. **Create an action plan and review it regularly.**

Set a deadline when you want to achieve your target. If your goal is a particularly challenging one, break it down into smaller, more manageable goals that culminate in attaining your main goal.

Rather than saying 'I want a promotion,' consider the smaller steps that will help get you to that goal. 'In the next four weeks, I will commit to taking on a project I haven't tried before.' Whatever you decide, ensure it is right for you.

3. **Make it specific and monitor your progress.**

How we articulate goals to ourselves is integral to the outcome of our efforts. Rather than a blanket statement, more specific goals will be much more effective. Rethink your objectives by presenting them in more specific terms, then build on that.

4. **Reward yourself for your successes, but don't punish yourself for failure.**

This doesn't mean rewarding yourself with chocolate when you attain a healthy eating goal, rather an internal pat on the back. Acknowledge your success and revel in the positive emotions that accompany it.

It is important to be resilient in the face of adversity. Reassess your goals and make alterations when you feel it is necessary to do so.

It's great to shoot for the stars, but goal setting is more about what you can realistically accomplish rather than an idealistic vision of what you hope you can achieve.

The old way used to be **SMART** goals.

**S**pecific
**M**easurable
**A**chievable
**R**ealistic
**T**ime-driven

I agree with most of it and would challenge the realistic. This is good for annual appraisals for employees. Bosses like to see their staff achieve their objectives, and staff like the feedback of achievement. But if they are realistic, will they stretch you enough?

You can't build muscles with a little exercise. That's not realistic. It takes training. I said earlier that a goal should be out of reach but not out of sight. Consider shooting for something that does not appear realistic and go for it. What's the worst-case scenario? You shoot for the stars but land on the moon.

When JFK told the world 'By the end of the decade, we will have a man on the moon,' that was not realistic. We didn't even have wheels on suitcases then. The computer capacity in your phone is far greater than that which was available to send astronauts to the moon. But they did it.

Sports athletes are breaking unrealistic records all the time, and guess what? Once they have achieved, many are not far behind. That's the other by-product of goals. They provide confidence and example for others to follow.

Maybe we change from realistic to relevant.

With our goals written down, what's next?

## Love your obstacles

For every goal, there will be obstacles, things in your way. What if they were removed, what's in your way now?

Dan Sullivan of Strategic Coach, one of the world's foremost experts on entrepreneurship in action, teaches us that 'our opportunities are in our obstacles.' He has specific tools and strategies for focussing on your obstacles.

Put simply, if you list your obstacles and develop a plan or strategy for their removal, this will massively complement your goals.

Here's what Dan thinks (and you're never too young to think like an entrepreneur):

*Most people don't seek out obstacles. It can be tough to get past them and daunting sometimes to even think about them.*

*For many entrepreneurs, though, obstacles are actually a necessity. They come up whenever we set big goals and create a big vision for the future. The key is not to avoid them, but to use them as an official and integral part of the solution.*

*What kinds of stories would we have to tell about our lives and careers if we didn't have obstacles to overcome and experiences to transform?*

*Where will the money come from? Wherever it is now?*

Here's a little hack I use all the time. This helps me focus on what I want and what's in my way, then very simply what I need to do.

### *Goal Buddy*

| | *Goal – Personal* | *What's in my way?* | *How do I remove what's in my way?* |
|---|---|---|---|
| 1 | 6 Riffs on my guitar by June | Commitment | 1. Book lessons with Zico<br>2. Allocate time to practise<br>3. Join a band |

| 2 | Drop 5 KG | • Lifestyle<br>• Work<br>• Movement | 1. Prep my own meals<br>2. No eating out for a month<br>3. No booze<br>4. Home exercise routine<br>5. 10,000 steps a day |
|---|---|---|---|
| 3 | Pass exams | Knowledge | • Get study materials<br>• Tutor<br>• Plan the time<br>• Get past papers |

## *How to Think through a Difficult Situation*

*In the Strategic Coach Program, we have a proprietary thinking tool called the Strategy Circle that allows anyone to transform obstacles and opposition into a strategic plan for reaching their goals. The thinking process behind it looks like this:*

*Step 1: Create a **vision**: Every important action always starts with a vision of somewhere you want to be in the future. Dream it, craft it, and write it down.*

*Step 2: Identify the **obstacles**: Allow yourself to think negatively and pinpoint all the opposition. Highlight everything that lies in between you and achieving your vision.*

*Step 3: Find **transformative** solutions: Face those obstacles one at a time and head on to find creative solutions and strategies to overcome them. Don't be afraid to ask for help. Others might be able to see a solution you can't.*

*Step 4: Take **action**. Now that you're fully prepared to move forward, get the resources you need to take the next step, and start making progress towards your goals.*

*After you've completed the process, you'll start over again. This is a constant activity you can do throughout your life to continually grow.*

*I have grown the most when I've been faced with difficulty.*
*—Dan Sullivan*

## Putting the Spotlight on Obstacles

*Having a big vision is the key to your entrepreneurial success—but you can't neglect the obstacles. Your vision will help you shed light on them, letting you see what you need to do to get to where you want to be.*

*A lot of people have trouble dealing with their obstacles when they simply think of them as general opposition, so the best thing to do is break the obstacles down into specific components. If you've determined that there are two or three things that need to be overcome, you know what you're facing and can figure out how to proceed one at a time.*

*Don't resist the opposition. If all our goals were easy and totally straightforward to achieve, we wouldn't have the opportunity to grow and improve. Obstacles shouldn't be avoided; they're there to help us get bigger and better and to raise our levels of capability and confidence, all whilst achieving our biggest goals and wildest dreams!'*

You also have some fun with this by thinking, what's great about this problem? What's funny about this problem? Go on, try. It could put you in a creative frame of mind to attack your obstacles. So embrace these obstacles as a good thing full of opportunities.

**Granddad Tip: Before you write your goals, ask yourself, are you serious or curious about achieving your goals?**

When the plan is in place, what's next?

## Inspect what you expect

Your brain loves feedback, so measure your progress. Be careful, though, because this will give you an endorphin rush. Yes, monitoring your own goals that are on track is a rush. You set the goal, you made the decision, and now like an architect, you can see the result of your planning. Enjoy this bit. It's all yours.

We know we need to monitor our goals because you can't manage what you don't measure. In fact, there's not much point in setting the goals if you don't measure your performance towards them.

Keep it flexible and allow things to change. Mike Tyson, the legendary world heavyweight boxer, said, 'Everyone has a plan until they get a punch in the face.' Expect a few punches. This is why many do not bother.

Monitoring your plan smashes shattered and cluttered thinking.

There are many positive side effects to this. Here are two massive questions:

1. Have you ever met anyone who has a great plan, is monitoring it, working towards their dreams and visions, and they are depressed?
2. Have you ever met anyone who is depressed, who has a great plan, is monitoring it, working towards their dreams and visions?

I appreciate there are times of psychological trauma and illness, but I haven't yet met anyone like this. There must be a powerful correlation.

By now, I hope you are thinking bigger and don't be frightened to look at the stars in awe because a head full of fears has no space for dreams.

Make your second home on the Goal Coast, and if the plan doesn't work, change the plan—never the goal.

**Granddad Tip: Consider an AGM with yourself. Once a year, when you are ready to set your goals, have a meeting with you.**

So this far, where is your pulse? Is it buzzing? I hope so. There's plenty more to come. Will this be day one or one day? It's your decision. You are in the driver's seat, not a passenger.

Now it's time to shape the right attitude and belief.

# 4

# How Will You React . . . To Everything?

*Thank your past for everything, for all your warts and all. Now get to work and fix your soul, and then achieve your goal.*

So much starts and sometimes ends right here: ATTITUDE.

Zig Ziglar said, 'It's not your aptitude but your attitude that determines your altitude.' So let's explore our attitude. This is *the* game-changer.

Attitude and personality are as important as experience and ability, but a bad attitude is like a flat tyre. You can't go anywhere until you change it.

I once worked with a former Special Air Service (SAS) soldier Daryll Hallett. Daryll was an instructor who assessed who would be selected to this elite regiment of the British forces. He actually has a mention in the book by Sir Ranulph Fiennes, OBE, *The Feather Men*.

A quiet family man with a calm demeanour, Daryll had nothing to prove to us, and he didn't try. I will always remember a small room in his farmhouse in West Wales that had every picture his children had drawn all over the four walls. I didn't have children then, but I hoped I could be as good as him as a dad.

SAS soldiers work in groups, usually consisting of four, with different skills and talents. Their job in wartime is to get behind enemy lines, disable assets, and provide intelligence. These are the elite but have to depend on one another.

One day, over lunch, I asked him many questions about this squad, which fascinated me. He would not betray any confidences but delighted me with the following story:

In those days, you had to be at least a sergeant in the army to be considered for the SAS. They were put through a grueling mission of selection in the Brecon Beacons. This included trekking across very severe terrain in the winter, carrying heavy artillery and supplies. The first group arrived. This group included a soldier who was a winner in every sense—fit, strong, and intelligent—and he wanted you to know it. He broke many records and expected to qualify with ease.

Many were sent out on the first exercise, and not all could make it to the end. Those who did returned to the finish base very tired, almost unable to walk. They would be met by Daryll who would give them their finishing time and tell them if they went through to the next stage. This was not a race. It was test of endurance, character, and attitude, but they didn't know that. One such soldier returned and was seriously tired and collapsed in a heap on the grass. He asked, barely able to speak, 'How did I do, sir?

This is the toughest exercise of my life. I can hardly breathe or talk. Was that more than 50 miles, sir?'

Daryll replied, 'Do it again, start again, and this time it's dark.'

The soldier rose to his feet, grabbed his sack and artillery, and made his way. After about a 10-metre hobble, Daryll called him back and said, 'Well done, you have passed.'

Daryll knew that this soldier could be relied upon and would not give up. His attitude was amazing. This was in sharp contrast to the winner who completed the course in record time. He too asked similar questions, and when he got the finish line, he got the same reply to do it again. He reacted, 'Why? I did it in record time. The best ever. What have I got to prove?'

Daryll told him, 'You have failed.'

This guy thought more of himself, his record and his ego. How could he be relied upon in an emergency? His attitude cost him the position despite his superior fitness.

This guy desperately needed an attitude adjustment.

Why not ask yourself, when in a situation that challenges your attitude, 'Am I getting bitter or better?'

A great example of someone who arguably should have been bitter is Nelson Mandela. He spent most of his adult life in prison in South Africa for political involvement. When he was released, he went on to be a popular president of South Africa.

Here's his example of a great attitude.

*After becoming president, I asked some of my bodyguard members to go for a walk in town. After the walk, we went for lunch at a restaurant. We sat in one of the most central ones, and each of us asked what we wanted. After a bit of waiting, the waiter, who brought our menus, appeared. At that moment, I realized that at the table that was right in front of ours, there was a single man waiting to be served.*

*When he was served, I told one of my soldiers, 'Go ask that man to join us.' The soldier went and transmitted my invitation. The man stood up, took the plate, and sat next to me. While eating, his hands were constantly shaking, and he didn't lift his head from the food. When we finished, he waved at me without even looking at me. I shook his hand and walked away!*

*The soldier said to me, 'Madiba, that man must be very sick as his hands wouldn't stop shaking while he was eating.'*

*'Not at all! The reason for his tremor is another,' I replied.*

*They looked at me weird, and I said to them, 'That man was the guardian of the jail I was locked up in. Often, after the torture I was subjected to, I screamed and cried for water, and he came to humiliate me, he laughed at me, and instead of giving me water, he urinated on my head.*

*'He wasn't sick, he was scared and shook, maybe fearing that I, now that I'm president of South Africa, would send him*

*to jail and do the same thing he did with me, torturing and humiliating him. But that's not me. That behaviour is not part of my character nor my ethics. Minds that seek revenge destroy states, while those that seek reconciliation build nations.'*
—Nelson Mandela

*You are never too old, it's never too late, and the choices you make will seal your fate.*

There are three choices: give up, give in, or give it all you got.

Let go of what you can't change. This will be a happy moment. Bad things will happen. You can either let it destroy you, define you, or strengthen you. Choose wisely.

We are what we pretend to be, so we must be careful about what we pretend to be. It isn't what you have or who you are or where you are or what you are doing that makes you happy or unhappy. It is what you think about. Positive thoughts are free, like smells, help yourself. Today's nice thoughts are on me.

***

Dronacharya called all his students for a test. They were asked to strike at the eye of a bird sitting on the top branch of a faraway tree.

Before the test commenced, he asked each student, 'What do you see?'

First one said, 'The tree, branches, leaves, bird, etc.'

Second one said, 'Sky, flying birds, leaves, bird, etc.'

Third one said, 'Bird and the branch beneath it.'

However, the fourth one said, 'I only see the eye of that bird.'

That student is Arjuna. He later went on to become one of the most skilful and strongest archers in Mahabharata.

Attitude is the ability to outthink others and have a different perspective, to aim for the cut above the rest, and train yourself to achieve it.

A positive attitude helps you cope more easily with the daily affairs of life. It brings optimism into your life and makes it easier to avoid worries and negative thinking. If you adopt it as a way of life, it would bring constructive changes into your life and makes them happier, brighter, and more successful.

Here's some giggle juice:

Maybe it starts with a smile because as Spike Milligan said,

>*Smiling is infectious*
>*You catch it like the flu.*
>*When someone smiled at me today*
>*I started smiling too.*
>*I walked around the corner*
>*And someone saw me grin.*
>*And when he smiled I realised*
>*I had passed it on to him.*
>*I thought about the smile*
>*And realised its worth.*
>*A single smile like mine*
>*Can travel round the earth.*
>*So if you see a smile begin*
>*Don't leave it undetected.*

*Start an epidemic
And get the world infected.*

\*\*\*

*An old man once said, 'Erasers are made
for those who make mistakes.'
The young lady replied, 'Erasers are made for those
who are willing to correct their mistakes.'*

**Attitude is everything.**

**Granddad Tip: Positive and negative emotions cannot occupy your mind at the same time. You know what to do.**

What's so interesting about the bonsai tree?

## Bonsai Trees

The object is not to make the tree look like the bonsai; it is to make the bonsai look like the tree.

The Japanese have a lovely hobby: cultivating bonsai trees, a process that includes cutting and pruning constantly until the tree is a dwarf tree, cut down to size and kept that way. What's that got to do with attitude? I know men who are over 6 feet tall who are dwarf men. They have been chipped away at all their life and accepted it. They have been told they are no good and now believe it. As beautiful as a bonsai tree is, it was conditioned for that in a beautiful way. That works both ways, positive and negative. DO NOT allow others to condition you by playing with your thinking. This affects your confidence and is voluntary. Confidence gets shattered with bad thinking. It can take years to cut down something beautiful to size and very hard to make it grow again.

I call bad thinking 'stinking thinking.' Stinking thinking takes you to a dark place. Do not let society chip away at you, cutting and pruning you down to an artificial size. Be more like the mighty oak tree that started life as a tiny acorn and let nothing stop your growth.

The vast majority of talk is self-talk. Be careful what you say to yourself. Think about it this way: You are the most influential person you will talk to today. The rest of your body is listening, and so is your mind. Both are ready to spring into action. Both will respond to what you are saying. This is exciting and dangerous.

Remember: It's better to light one candle than to curse the darkness.

*Be the change you want to be in the world.*

Some fear success. Why would they do that? Let's talk about success.

## Don't Be Afraid to Succeed

*If you don't fight for what you want, don't cry for what you lost.*

Sometimes people's greatest fear is success. We know fear of failure, but fear of success is real. Some feel they are not worth it. It could take them out of their comfort zone. Will they have to mix with different people? What will their friends and family think? Will this be comfortable? Will I have to learn new skills and capabilities? All important questions.

The disbeliever has a fear of success that is manifesting itself when they fight change or can justify why things can't change. You will hear them say, 'We don't do it like that,' 'It can't be done,' 'That would never work.' This pessimism is dangerous.

> *The pessimist sees the difficulty in every opportunity while the optimist sees the opportunity in every difficulty.*
> —Sir Winston Churchill

Let me tell you about the bamboo tree. The bamboo tree, when planted, does nothing visible for the first five years. It then grows 80 feet in six months. You think nothing is happening. It's establishing roots. Then nature takes over. Same in life. Build the most important part of your life—your roots. Then when you grow 80 feet, don't be surprised when luck finds you.

Success is not to be feared, nor are the new lifestyle and new capabilities. This will help you grow.

You do not have to be fearful of trying something new. Remember: Amateurs built the *Ark*. Professionals built the *Titanic*.

\*\*\*

And you don't always have to go far to find it. One of my favourite stories is 'Acres of Diamonds.'

It's a favourite because of the principles revealed. Based on a true story, it has been told with many versions.

Years ago, when the first diamonds were being discovered in Africa, diamond fever spread across the continent like wildfire. Many people struck it rich in their search for the sparkling beauties, and they became millionaires overnight.

At this time, Lamar, a young black farmer in Central Africa, was scratching out a moderate living on the land that he owned. However, the promise of great diamond wealth soon possessed Lamar, and one day he could no longer restrain his insatiable desire for diamonds and the lust to become a wealthy man. He sold his farm, packed a few essentials, and left his family in search of the magnificent stones.

His search was long and painful. He wandered throughout the African continent, fighting insects and wild beasts, sleeping in the elements, fighting the damp and cold. Lamar searched day after day, week after week, but found no diamonds. He became sick, penniless, and utterly discouraged. He felt there was nothing more to live for, so he threw himself in a raging river and drowned.

Meanwhile, back on the farm that Lamar had sold, the farmer who bought the land was working the soil one day and found a strange-looking stone in the small creek that ran across the farm. The farmer brought it in to his farmhouse and placed it on the fireplace mantle as a curio.

Later a visitor came to the farmer's home and noticed the unusual stone. He grasped the stone quickly and shouted excitedly at the farmer, 'Do you know this is a diamond? It's one of the largest diamonds I've ever seen.'

Further investigation revealed that the entire farm was covered with magnificent diamonds. In fact, this farm turned out to be one of the richest and most productive diamond mines in the world, and the farmer became one of the wealthiest men in Africa.

How sad that Lamar had not taken the time to investigate what he had right at his own fingertips. Instead, he gave up everything he had in search of wealth that was right under his nose.

The seeds of opportunity usually are inherent in what we already know and are already doing. Don't think 'the grass is greener on the other side of the fence' or that you must start something totally new and different to become successful. Just do what you already know 10 percent better or provide added value.

Love what you have. The grass is only greener where you water it.

Now have the courage to be disliked. Take and give, not give and take.

If it's money you want, I believe you are a millionaire. You just haven't had the money yet.

You won't regret most of what you've done, but you will regret all of what you didn't do.

The Maharishi Mahesh Yogi, an Indian guru, was once asked, 'Where will I get the money from?'

'From wherever it is now,' he answered.

No matter how bad things are today, tomorrow is a wonderful opportunity to change it and make it better, but realise that fear is not real. It is created by your thinking. Do not misunderstand me, danger is real, but fear is a choice you make.

Another fear is that success requires you to be extreme because moderation is the recipe for mediocrity, the exception being your diet.

You don't have to look out of the window, just the mirror.

Get over it, get through it, get on with it.

Did you know that you can't become who you want to be if you're too attached to who you used to be?

Turn your cant's into cans and your dreams into plans.

In Susan Jeffers's book, *Feel the Fear and Do It Anyway*, she quotes, 'A ship in its harbor is safe, but a ship wasn't built for that.' A ship was built to brave the seven seas in good or bad weather, just like you.

You can do this because

*You can be a total winner,*
*Even if you're a beginner,*
*If you think you can, you can*
*If you think you can, you can.*
*Raise that C up to an A*
*Get in that school play*
*If you think you can.*
*It's not your talent or a gifted birth*
*It's not your bank book that determines worth*
*It isn't even the color or the texture of your skin*
*It's your attitude that makes you win.*
*You can wear the gold medallion*
*You can ride your own black stallion*
*You can profit through inflation*
*You can redirect this nation*
*If you think you can*
*Doesn't matter if you won before*
*Makes no difference what's the half-time score*
*It's never over till the final gun, Is there one?*
*You keep on trying, you'll find you've won.*
*Now grab your dream and then believe it*
*Get to work, you'll achieve it*
*If you think you can you can.*
*If you think you can you can.*
—Dr Dennis Waitley

No matter how bad things are today, tomorrow is a wonderful opportunity to change it and make it better.

*Heroes are made by the path they choose,*
*not powers they are graced with.*
—Iron Man

Next, shall we go looking for monsters? They are very close.

## Monster Me

*Don't get stuck in your own head.*

The best time to kill a monster is when it's young. Want to go to prison? The scariest prison is in your mind, so let's do a jailbreak. There are mental monsters lurking away in the depths of your mind. They don't belong there, and they are not paying rent, so let's evict them. You cannot be free until you free yourself from the prison of your own false thoughts.

The term *positive thinking* has become devalued by overuse. Everyone is a psychologist on social media, and many regurgitate others' quotes (including me). When you have too much of something, you can get complacent and not appreciate the value of *good thinking*.

Mental monsters, horror movies from the past or worse still worrying about things that have not happened.

This is an example of stinking thinking. The only difference between a rut and a grave is the depth, and stinking thinking is the shovel that digs your grave.

***

The two wolves. There's a great short story told by the Native American Indian tribes. They say that inside of all of us are two wolves. One is kind, loving, and helpful. The other is nasty, aggressive, and dangerous. Which one wins? The one you feed. You feed them with your thoughts, so be careful about what you think.

Some of this is triggered by feelings of lack, and that is a decision you take. We will cover that later.

Another mental monster is worry. The best way to overcoming worry is great clean thinking.

You need to be around the right people and in the right environment and don't believe everything you think. Your brain is trying to protect you and will tell you not to take the risk. I do believe when you get great people together, amazing things happen.

Get around the right people. Avoid negative people at all costs. They will not share your dreams, which is why they are negative. In fact, they will take pleasure in spoiling your dreams. So before we move on, think of who they are now and ditch them from your life.

Did you do it? How does that feel?

There's a war in your head. Let's win a few battles.

Who would you prefer to be around—someone pretending to be positive or someone who is sincerely negative?

Learn to deal with things as they arrive, rather than worrying them into existence. Life is too short to spend it at war with yourself.

Too many are not living their dreams, living their failures, and need to rationalise it by bringing you down too. It justifies their negativity.

> *Bad thoughts take space in a beautiful place—*
> *your head, your heart, your gut.*
> *If you fill that space with action and pace,*
> *you will always avoid that rut.*

We can't win in life if we're losing in our mind, so change your thoughts and you can change your world. Remember, you spend most of your life in your head. Make sure it's a beautiful place.

There may be times when you feel in a dark place, and it feels like you've been buried. Maybe you haven't been buried. Maybe you've have been planted.

It takes the exact same amount of time and energy to imagine great things as it does to worry. The results are incredibly different. So instead of saying, 'Why is this happening to me?' ask yourself, 'What is this teaching me?'

**Granddad Tip: You will meet many people who are frightened to die, but sadly, there are far more who are frightened to live. They make their monsters real. Help these lost souls. Sprinkle some of your magic on them. They need you.**

*You will never reach your destination if you stop
and throw stones at every dog that barks.*
—*Churchill*

What else can help with great clean thinking?

Next up, let's shine some light on belief.

## Do You Believe . . . In You?

The only difference between a big shot and a little shot is that a big shot was once a little shot who didn't stop shooting.

This is why so many give up. They stop shooting. Keep on keeping on. The world is full of inspirational stories of people who overcame enormous obstacles but made it.

All big dreams have small beginnings. I am always amazed by how many sports men and women at the top of their game started with failures. Same in business.

What if you can? How do you know you can't?

Now you can go beyond the dream and make it an intention. Then take it back to goals and vision. Can you see how you can jump around this book and strategies to get on or back on track?

When you feel like you are not enough, you seek external validation from others. This can let the rot in at a bad vulnerable time. You are enough.

You already have the talent, skills, and ability to succeed, but do you have the guts to fail? Failure is an option. Failure is badly labeled. Failure is feedback, and all the greats have failed their way to the top.

Sometimes you have these 'seek-and-destroy viruses' in your head. What's the job of a virus? Seek and destroy. Do not allow this. The best medicine is good thinking.

Small minds will try and convince you that your dreams are too big. They are right. Your dreams are too big for *them*. What others think of you is irrelevant. Don't let someone else's opinion of you become your reality. It's often their problem. Let them own it.

Stay strong. There's always a rainbow after the storm.

> *Everyone wants to be happy,*
> *Nobody wants any pain,*
> *But you can't have a nice rainbow*
> *Without plenty of rain.*

No matter how bad things are today, tomorrow is a wonderful opportunity to change it and make it better. Your bad times give you all the knowledge that your soul cannot.

Get over it, get through it, get on with it.

## Limiting Beliefs

Belief is a very powerful force, even if it's false. Here are a few examples:

### *The Barracuda and the Little Fish*

Many years ago, a team studied the effects of belief. They placed a large barracuda and a small fish in a tank. The barracuda would always swoop up to the fish and swallow it whole. After a while, they put a glass panel between them. The barracuda would still go for the fish, but now it kept hitting its head. It didn't know the wall was there. After a while, they removed the glass panel.

The barracuda would still swim towards the fish but stop short at the point where the panel was. It still believed that this now imaginary wall was there. It acted on false information and genuinely believed it would be hurt if it went further. This is a limiting belief that's not real but so powerful.

### *The Circus Elephant*

You have probably seen in the movies or maybe at the circus how big and strong elephants are.

You will have noticed that this huge beast is usually chained to a stump of wood in the ground. He could easily pull the stump out but doesn't. Why? When the elephant is young, they tie its leg to the stump. It is not strong enough to remove it as a calf, but after years of conditioning, it believes it is stuck and does not try to escape. How dangerous is that? You have the ability to break free, but you do not believe and are, therefore, trapped.

## *Placebos*

Doctors will often prescribe pills that contain nothing. These are for people who believe they are ill, and they are not. When these patients take the pills, they believe they are cured or that the pills are helping. They were not ill, so how could they be cured? This is scary—people being cured from an illness they didn't have by pills that contain nothing. All made up in the head.

Do not let this influence your thinking or state.

Did you know that . . .

> All the water in the world,
> However hard you tried,
> Could never, ever, sink a ship,
> unless it got inside.
>
> All the evil in the world,
> The wickedness and sin,
> Can never sink your soul's fair craft,
> Unless you let it in.
> All the hardships of this world
> Might wear you pretty thin,
> But they won't hurt you one least bit,
> Unless you let them in.
> *There is no downside to believing in yourself.*

How do we deal with grief?

# Dealing with Grief

Grief comes in many forms, usually if you lose someone special. If you're feeling grief, they must have been important to you.

It will be hard to watch anything positive or have good thoughts in the early stages of grief.

Sometimes thoughts will come out of your mind and run down your cheeks.

The pain of grief can often cause you to want to withdraw from others and retreat into your shell. But having the face-to-face support of other people is vital to healing from loss. Even if you're not comfortable talking about your feelings under normal circumstances, it's important to express them when you're grieving. Whilst sharing your loss can make the burden of grief easier to carry, that doesn't mean that every time you interact with friends and family, you need to talk about your loss. Comfort can also come from just being around others who care about you. The key is not to isolate yourself.

The best way I deal with this is make the grief a celebration of the lost loved one's life. It's not easy, but everyone I've loved and lost would have wanted that.

One of the things the Irish do well is wakes. Coming from Irish descendants, I went to many. It was hard to grieve when everyone was telling stories about the person we lost. It had an amazing feeling of adding sense to a sad occasion when it was not considered good to make this a happy time. We can learn so much from this.

Always remember the good times and include some funny times.

If they could, they would be grateful and talking about gratitude. One phrase I get comfort from when grieving is

*This too shall pass.*

Are you grateful?

## Why Is It Important to Be Grateful?

*Life may not be the party we hoped for, but we are here now, so we might as well dance.*

Grateful people are happy people. Ungrateful people are *always* miserable. That's why they are miserable. They are not satisfied with what they have and are constantly looking for more.

Don't confuse this with ambition. That's healthy, but on the way, we must be grateful for what we have.

Develop an attitude of gratitude.

*The roots of all goodness lie in the soul of appreciation.*
—*Dalai Lama*

Your body is so sophisticated. Your eyes are better than any camera invented. Your ears are amazing. Your brain is more sophisticated than any computer, and we still do not know its full potential.

Often the things we have right now are things we dreamt about in the past. Let's be grateful.

Don't let an insatiable desire for more blind you from seeing and appreciating everything you have right now. You have far more than you know. Be grateful.

Remember also that so many people want you to succeed. Your life touches so many others, and many are rooting for you.

A very welcome by-product of gratitude is that it kills anger. Try it out, it works like magic. It's hard to be angry when you are grateful.

Maintain an attitude of gratitude. It will make you feel good.

Someone once said, 'The struggle ends when the gratitude begins.'

Now march forward feeling proud like a beautiful horse, *clippety clop, clippety clop.*

## Clippety Clop, Clippety Clop

Look proud, trim that mane, tail all bushy, you are the star. When you're brimming with confidence, you can unleash your wild on your life, and it's great to have a wild side.

Beauty is holding your head up high and being you. People can copy a lot about you, but they cannot copy your vibe—that's unique to you.

A little girl named Jen normally kept her head held low, as she felt she wasn't pretty enough. One day she went to a jewellery store and bought a red bow. The owner kept telling her how pretty she looked with her brand new bow. Jen was very happy and held her head up high. She wanted everyone to see her new bow. When someone bumped into her, she hardly noticed it.

When she walked into her classroom, the teacher said, 'Jen, you look so pretty when your head is held up high!' Her teacher even gave her a little hug.

She received a lot of praise that day, which, of course, she had attributed to her new bow. However, when she looked in the mirror, she couldn't find the bow. She concluded that the bow must've fallen off her head when someone bumped into her.

Self-confidence is a form of beauty; however, most people think that beauty lies in appearances. It's a big reason why so many people are unhappy these days. It doesn't matter if you're rich or poor, pretty or plain, as long as you can hold your head up high, you'll feel happy, which, in turn, makes you look charming and lovely.

Charlie Chaplin read this poem by Kim McMillen on the occasion of his seventieth birthday. What's wrong with loving yourself?

### As I Began to Love Myself

As I began to love myself
I found that anguish and emotional suffering

are only warning signs that I was living
against my own truth.
Today, I know, this is Authenticity.
As I began to love myself
I understood how much it can offend somebody
if I try to force my desires on this person,
even though I knew the time was not right
and the person was not ready for it,
and even though this person was me.
Today I call this Respect.
As I began to love myself
I stopped craving for a different life,
and I could see that everything
that surrounded me
was inviting me to grow.
Today I call this Maturity.
As I began to love myself
I understood that at any circumstance,
I am in the right place at the right time,
and everything happens at the exactly right moment.
So I could be calm.
Today I call this Self-Confidence.
As I began to love myself
I quit stealing my own time,
and I stopped designing huge projects
for the future.
Today, I only do what brings me joy and happiness,
things I love to do and that make my heart cheer,
and I do them in my own way
and in my own rhythm.
Today I call this Simplicity.
As I began to love myself

I freed myself of anything
that is no good for my health—
food, people, things, situations,
and everything that drew me down
and away from myself.
At first I called this attitude a healthy egoism.
Today I know it is Love of Oneself.
As I began to love myself
I quit trying to always be right,
and ever since
I was wrong less of the time.
Today I discovered that is Modesty.
As I began to love myself
I refused to go on living in the past
and worrying about the future.
Now, I only live for the moment,
where everything is happening.
Today I live each day,
day by day,
and I call it Fulfilment.
As I began to love myself
I recognized
that my mind can disturb me
and it can make me sick.
But as I connected it to my heart,
my mind became a valuable ally.
Today I call this connection Wisdom of the Heart.
We no longer need to fear arguments,
confrontations or any kind of problems
with ourselves or others.
Even stars collide,

and out of their crashing, new worlds are born.
Today I know: This is Life!

*When you feel like you want to take on the rest of the world, dress like you are going to meet your worst enemy today.*
—Coco Chanel

I wouldn't argue with Coco.

If you look lovely, you will attract the attention of others, but try and avoid the gossip and the chitchat.

## Chitter Chatter, Chitter Chatter, Chit, Chit, Chit

*Gossip—the toxic habit for those with poor tacky character.*

Gossip is largely about insecurities. Some feel a pleasure in talking about others. This is a trap. If they talk to you about others, you can rest assured they are talking about you to others too.

*Anyone who will gossip to you will gossip about you.*

Insecure people love this. It takes the emphasis from their failures. They like nothing more than a pity party and are usually backward-thinking people. Let them live in the past, or you could be dragged back there with them.

Work on the destruction of drama—their drama. Don't be afraid to speak up about this to the drama kings and queens. If you don't feed their habit, they will stop. Mission accomplished.

That's the way to destroy this very negative attribute and keep the conversation respectful. I guarantee this will earn you respect.

You can't grow to like people who gossip behind your back because that's exactly where they belong—behind your back.

Sometimes it's not their fault. Some of them are lost, disillusioned, and hurt.

They have no worth and feel better when others fail and are down and broken, so they advertise it.

**Granddad Tip: Don't attend or participate in pity parties.**

Can you hear them?

**Listening**

Listening is a skill I learnt later in life. My mind works quickly, and I often found myself finishing people's sentences. I thought I knew what they going say from the early stage of our conversation.

This is rude and does not show respect. This is when I realised that I had two ears and one mouth. Maybe nature is telling us something.

There is a power in silence. Silence is not empty. It's full of answers. Silence is often the best answer.

Have you noticed that *silent* and *listen* are made up of the same letters? Think about that.

Moving forward, now to form some good habits.

# 5

# Habits

*First, you make your habits, and then your habits make you.*

Good habits give you energy for the entire day. They make a massive contribution to the life you are building and your personal happiness.

Wherever you are right now, it's as a result of your habits, good or bad.

It doesn't take long to change your life with habits, good or bad.

There are no extraordinary people in the world, only extraordinary habits.

I read it takes twenty-one days to create a habit that sticks, that's all. So in a year, you can create many new good habits.

Bad habits often come from stress and boredom and need to be replaced. What's your escape route?

Break those habits that can break you. Adopt those practises that will become the new habits that will help you achieve the success you desire.

This is a great way to protect your confidence, and you will hear me many times talking about the importance of protecting your confidence. Your confidence is the electricity that flows through your body and energises you. Protect it at all times. When you build strong habits, you don't have to rely on motivation.

You will always ooze confidence from the promises you made and kept to yourself.

How do we create good habits? Let's start now by visiting one of the best.

Stephen Covey, in his highly-successful book, *The 7 Habits of Highly Successful People*, stated these magnificent seven (here is a great summary by Anum Hussain):

1. **Be Proactive**

Put simply, to be effective, we must be proactive.

Reactive people take a passive stance. They believe the world is happening to them. They say things like:

- 'There's nothing I can do.'
- 'That's just the way I am.'

They think the problem is 'out there'—that thought is the problem.

Reactivity becomes a self-fulfilling prophecy, and reactive people feel increasingly victimised and out of control.

Proactive people, however, recognise they have responsibility—or 'response-ability,' which Covey defines as the ability to choose how you will respond to a situation.

2. **Begin with the End in Mind**

Start with a clear vision in mind. Covey says we can use our imagination to develop a vision of what we want to become and use our conscience to decide what values will guide us.

Most of us find it rather easy to busy ourselves. We work hard to achieve victories: promotions, higher income, more recognition. But we don't often stop to evaluate the meaning behind this busyness, behind these victories. We don't ask ourselves if these things that we focus on so intently are what really matter to us.

Habit 2 suggests that, in everything we do, we should begin with the end in mind. Start with a clear destination. That way, we can make sure the steps we're taking are in the right direction.

Covey emphasises that our self-awareness empowers us to shape our own lives, instead of living our lives by default or based on the standards or preferences of others.

Beginning with the end in mind is also extremely important for businesses. Being a manager is about optimising for efficiency. But being a leader is about setting the right strategic vision for your organisation in the first place and asking, 'What are we trying to accomplish?'

Before we as individuals or organisations can start setting and achieving goals, we must be able to identify our values. This process may involve some rescripting to be able to assert our own personal values.

Rescripting, Covey explains, is recognising ineffective scripts that have been written for you and changing those scripts by proactively writing new ones that are built of your own values.

It is also important to identify our centre. Whatever is at the centre of our life will be the source of our security, guidance, wisdom, and power.

Our centres affect us fundamentally. They determine our daily decisions, actions, and motivations, as well as our interpretation of events.

However, Covey notes that none of these centres are optimal and that, instead, we should strive to be principle-centred. We should identify the timeless, unchanging principles by which we must live our lives. This will give us the guidance that we need to align our behaviours with our beliefs and values.

### 3. **Put First Things First**

To manage ourselves effectively, we must put first things first. We must have the discipline to prioritise our day-to-day actions based on what is most important, not what is most urgent.

Habit 3 is about actually going after these goals and executing on our priorities on a day-to-day, moment-to-moment basis.

To maintain the discipline and the focus to stay on track towards our goals, we need to have the willpower to do something when we don't want to do it. We need to act according to our values rather than our desires or impulses at any given moment.

All activities can be categorised based on two factors: urgent and important.

## 4. Think Win-Win

To establish effective <u>interdependent relationships</u>, we must commit to creating win-win situations that are mutually beneficial and satisfying to each party.

Covey explains that there are six paradigms of human interaction:

1. Win-Win: Both people win. Agreements or solutions are mutually beneficial and satisfying to both parties.

2. Win-Lose: 'If I win, you lose.' Win-Lose people are prone to use position, power, credentials, and personality to get their way.

3. Lose-Win: 'I lose, you win.' Lose-Win people are quick to please and appease and seek strength from popularity or acceptance.

4. Lose-Lose: Both people lose. When two Win-Lose people get together—that is, when two determined, stubborn, ego-invested individuals interact—the result will be Lose-Lose.

5. Win: People with the Win mentality don't necessarily want someone else to lose—that's irrelevant. What matters is that they get what they want.

6. Win-Win or No Deal: If you can't reach an agreement that is mutually beneficial, there is no deal.

The best option is to create win-win situations. With win-lose or lose-win, one person appears to get what he wants for the moment, but the results will negatively impact the relationship between those two people going forward.

The win-win or no-deal option is important to use as a backup. When we have no-deal as an option in our mind, it liberates us from needing to manipulate people and push our own agenda. We can be open and really try to understand the underlying issues.

In solving for win-win, we must consider two factors: consideration and courage.

Another important factor in solving for win-win situations is maintaining an abundance mentality or the belief that there's plenty out there for everyone.

Most people operate with the scarcity mentality—meaning they act as though everything is zero-sum (in other words, if you get it, I don't). People with the scarcity mentality have a very hard time sharing recognition or credit and find it difficult to be genuinely happy about other people's successes.

When it comes to interpersonal leadership, the more genuine our character is, the higher our level of proactivity; the more committed we are to win-win, the more powerful our influence will be.

To achieve win-win, keep the focus on results, not methods; on problems, not people.

The spirit of win-win can't survive in an environment of competition. As an organisation, we need to align our reward system with our goals and values and have the systems in place to support win-win.

## 5. Seek First to Understand Then to Be Understood

Before we can offer advice, suggest solutions, or effectively interact with another person in any way, we must seek to deeply understand them and their perspective through empathic listening.

Let's say you go to an optometrist and tell him that you've been having trouble seeing clearly, and he takes off his glasses, hands them to you, and says, 'Here, try these—they've been working for me for years!'

You put them on, but they only make the problem worse. What are the chances you'd go back to that optometrist?

Unfortunately, we do the same thing in our everyday interactions with others. We prescribe a solution before we diagnose the problem. We don't seek to deeply understand the problem first.

Habit 5 says that we must seek first to understand, then to be understood. To seek to understand, we must learn to listen.

To listen empathically requires a fundamental paradigm shift. We typically seek first to be understood. Most people listen with the intent to reply, not to understand. At any given moment, they're either speaking or preparing to speak.

After all, Covey points out, communication experts estimate that

- 10 percent of our communication is represented by our words
- 30 percent is represented by our sounds

- 60 percent is represented by our body language

When we listen autobiographically—in other words, with our own perspective as our frame of reference—we tend to respond in one of four ways:

1. Evaluate: Agree or disagree with what is said
2. Probe: Ask questions from our own frame of reference
3. Advise: Give counsel based on our own experience
4. Interpret: Try to figure out the person's motives and behaviour based on our own motives and behaviour

But if we replace these types of response with empathic listening, we see dramatic results in improved communication. It takes time to make this shift, but it doesn't take nearly as long to practise empathic listening as it does to back up and correct misunderstandings or to live with unexpressed and unresolved problems only to have them surface later on.

The second part of habit 5 is 'then to be understood.' This is equally critical in achieving win-win solutions.

When we're able to present our ideas clearly, and in the context of a deep understanding of the other person's needs and concerns, we significantly increase the credibility of your ideas.

## 6. Synergise

By understanding and valuing the differences in another person's perspective, we have the opportunity to create synergy, which allows us to uncover new possibilities through openness and creativity.

The combination of all the other habits prepares us for habit 6, which is the habit of synergy or 'when one plus one equals three or more and the whole is greater than the sum of its parts.' For example, if you plant two plants close together, their roots will commingle and improve the quality of the soil so that both plants will grow better than they would on their own.

<u>Synergy</u> allows us to create new alternatives and open new possibilities. It allows us as a group to collectively agree to ditch the old scripts and write new ones.

So how can we introduce synergy to a given situation or environment? Start with habits 4 and 5—you must think win-win and seek first to understand.

Once you have these in mind, you can pool your desires with those of the other person or group. And then you're not on opposite sides of the problem—you're together on one side, looking at the problem, understanding all the needs, and working to create a third alternative that will meet them.

What we end up with is not a transaction but a transformation. Both sides get what they want, and they build their relationship in the process.

You are putting forth a spirit of trust and safety that will prompt others to become extremely open and feed on one another's insights and ideas, creating synergy.

The real essence of synergy is valuing the differences—the mental, emotional, and psychological differences amongst people.

After all, if two people have the same opinion, one is unnecessary. When we become aware of someone's different perspective, we can say, 'Good! You see it differently! Help me see what you see.'

We seek first to understand, and then we find strength and utility in those different perspectives to create new possibilities and win-win results.

Synergy allows you to

- Value the differences in other people as a way to expand your perspective
- Sidestep negative energy and look for the good in others
- Exercise courage in interdependent situations to be open and encourage others to be open
- Catalyse creativity and find a solution that will be better for everyone by looking for a third alternative

7. **Sharpen the Saw**

To be effective, we must devote the time to renewing ourselves physically, spiritually, mentally, and socially. Continuous renewal allows us to synergistically increase our ability to practise each habit.

Habit 7 is focussed on renewal or taking time to 'sharpen the saw.' It surrounds all the other habits and makes each one possible by preserving and enhancing your greatest asset—yourself.

There are four dimensions of our nature, and each must be exercised regularly and in balanced ways:

Physical Dimension: The goal of continuous physical improvement is to exercise our body in a way that will enhance our capacity to work, adapt, and enjoy.

To renew ourselves physically, we must:

- Eat well
- Get sufficient rest and relaxation
- Exercise on a regular basis to build endurance, flexibility, and strength

Focussing on the physical dimension helps develop habit 1 muscles of proactivity. We act based on the value of well-being, instead of reacting to the forces that keep us from fitness.

Spiritual Dimension: The goal of renewing our spiritual self is to provide leadership to our life and reinforce your commitment to our value system.

To renew yourself spiritually, you can

- Practise daily meditation
- Communicate with nature
- Immerse yourself in great literature or music

A focus on our spiritual dimension helps us practise habit 2 as we continuously revise and commit ourselves to our values so we can begin with the end in mind.

Mental Dimension: The goal of renewing our mental health is to continue expanding our mind.

To renew yourself mentally, you can

- Read good literature
- Keep a journal of your thoughts, experiences, and insights
- Limit television watching to only those programs that enrich your life and mind

Focussing on our mental dimension helps us practise habit 3 by managing ourselves effectively to maximise the use of our time and resources.

Social/Emotional Dimension: The goal of renewing ourselves socially is to develop meaningful relationships.

To renew yourself emotionally, you can

- Seek to deeply understand other people
- Make contributions to meaningful projects that improve the lives of others
- Maintain an abundance mentality and seek to help others find success

Renewing our social and emotional dimension helps us practise habits 4, 5, and 6 by recognising that win-win solutions do exist, seeking to understand others, and finding mutually-beneficial third alternatives through synergy.

As we focus on renewing ourselves along these four dimensions, we must also seek to be a positive scripter for other people. We must look to inspire others to a higher path by showing them we believe in them, by listening to them empathically, by encouraging them to be proactive.

The real beauty of the seven habits is that improvement in one habit synergistically increases our ability to improve the rest.

Renewal is the process that empowers us to move along an upward spiral of growth and change, of continuous improvement.

These are great habits and a great way to live your life by. They include different thinking, and good thinking is an addiction, a good addiction as opposed to stinking thinking.

What habits do the best adopt?

Building strong habits leaves you less dependent on depending on motivation.

What habits do you need to make you happy and successful?

Let's look at some habits of highly-successful people and see if we can learn from them.

1. They take full responsibility for their life.

They do not blame others. They take the credit and the blame.

2. They prioritise and do the most important things first.

They distinguishing the important and the urgent.

3. They create their own morning routine.

This is their personal ritual to get going.

4. They practise daily meditation or mindfulness.

This is to keep them calm and focussed.

5. They make health and exercise a priority.

This is to keep them energised for the excitement ahead.

6. They read and learn continuously.

This is to keep them contemporary.

7. They have great discipline and self-control.

They are in charge.

8. They are consistent.

They do not waver.

9. They focus on results and follow through on what they say with *no* excuses.

This makes them dependable.

10. They persevere with persistence.

They are totally focussed and not giving up.

11. They are not afraid to fail.

They treat failure as feedback, valuable feedback.

12. They hone their craft and sharpen their saw.

They are always learning and improving.

13. They are very aware of themselves.

They are comfortable in their own skin and not trying to be someone else.

14. They are grateful.

They see gratitude as a strength.

15. They have a support system.

They have a good team and are good team players—win-win.

16. They surround themselves with like-minded people.

'Birds of a feather flock together,' even the bad ones.

17. They are very goal-oriented.

Their goals and their dreams are their focus.

18. They are proactive, and they take initiative.

They are leading from the front and not waiting to be told.

19. They manage their emotions.

They are composed and controlled.

20. They communicate clearly.

They are simple and effective.

21. They are good listeners.

They believe that God gave us two ears and one mouth is a message.

22. They value time alone.

They are not afraid of their own company and use the time to plan and reflect.

23. They love the journey more than the result.

All part of their plan, to enjoy it on the way. The result is then more enjoyable.

24. They recognise what didn't work.

And they learn from it.

25. They plan.

It's their plan.

26. They do one thing at a time.

If you chase two rabbits, they both get away.

Did you notice how many of Stephen Covey's habits appear here?

Your morning ritual or routine, is this going to be a millionaire morning?

Starting your day right is so important. Here are a few suggestions:

- Wake up early.
- Drink water.
- Write things down.
- Read.
- Practise mindfulness.
- Stretch or exercise.
- Eat a healthy breakfast.
- Express gratitude.
- Say your affirmations.
- Connect with loved ones.
- Ask yourself important questions—my favourite 'I wonder.'
- Get the crap out of the way early.

These are ideas around good habits. Don't forget how easy it is to fall into the trap of bad habits. It's so easy to be complacent. Bad habits come from stress and boredom; they need to be replaced. What's your escape route? Use the above in your plan towards great habits.

But don't go over the top. You can

> Dust if you must, but wouldn't it be better
> To paint a picture or write a letter,
> Bake a cake or plant a seed,
> Ponder the difference between want and need.
> Dust if you must, but there's not much time

With rivers to swim and mountains to climb,
Music to hear and books to read,
Friends to cherish and a life to lead.
Dust if you must, but the world's out there
With the sun in your eyes and the wind in your hair
A flutter of snow, a shower of rain.
This day will not come around again.
Dust if you must, but bear in mind,
Old age will come, and it's not kind,
And when you go, and go you must,
You yourself will make more *dust*.

Next up, the right habits need good focus. Let's focus on focus, come on.

# 6

# Focus

Focus on results. Just 212 degrees are required to boil an egg. Anything above that is wasted energy.
—Tim Ferris

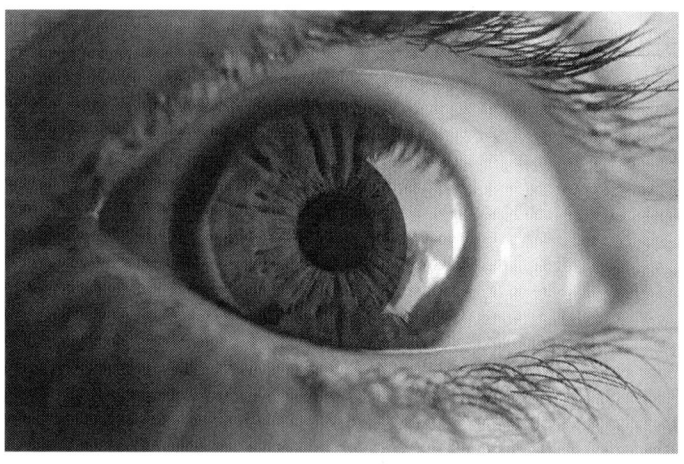

You don't run out of ideas. You run out of focus. It's time to get focussed.

In our chapter on belief, I said the only difference between a big shot and a little shot is that a big shot was once a little shot who didn't stop shooting. That little shot was focussed, and nothing was going to stop him. He learnt to sharpen the lens and narrow the focus, not widen the lens and blur the focus.

He didn't take a shotgun (scattered) approach to his goals. He took a rifle and honed in on them, picking them off in order of priority.

I mentioned in 'Habits' that if you chase two rabbits, both will get away. This is why you need to focus.

The technique here is to filter out all non-essential activities when required, and then you are only left with focus on the right activities.

Many top athletes and businesspeople talk about being in the zone and flow. Flow follows deep focus.

Not all zones are good. There's also comfort zones and danger zones. Focus gets you out of these. The comfort zones can and often do become the danger zones.

I'm not talking about perfection. Perfection kills creativity. I'm talking about the right amount of time being allocated to the right activities, whether you feel like it or not, keeping all distractions at bay and concentrating on the job in hand.

What's your perfect day? Focus on that and then ask yourself, 'Why not every day?'

To help you focus, try a to-do list and a not-to-do list. This will help concentration and draw attention to the things that you shouldn't be doing.

What is your number 1 success blocker? Usually, it's entertainment or social media. Decide to put that away during your golden hours, yours focus hours.

Instead of fixing your problems, try to fix your thinking and watch with joy how the problems fix themselves. That's focus.

Be brilliant at the basics.

- There are only seven colours, but look what Michelangelo did.
- There's only seven musical notes, but look what Mozart did.
- There are only ten numbers, but look what Copernicus did.

You can't make more time, but you can make more of the time you have. And time is all you have. So don't count time. Make time count.

Hard work works but must be focussed, or you will be a busy fool.

If you can't spend time on motivation, spend it on design. Design gets you creative, gets your juices flowing.

Things may not get easier, but you will get faster at everything.

Getting things done creates powerful personal productivity, which flows through focus.

Did you hear the famous quote from Lee Trevino, the famous golfer, when he was told he was lucky? He said, 'The harder I work, the luckier I get.' He was a champion— a focussed champion.

When you are focussed, you keep your eyes on the prize. Now get your eyes on the prize, and that prize is you. When you focus on you, you grow. When you focus on crap, crap grows. Read that again.

**Granddad Tip: Work backwards from possibility to creation.**

Did I tell you about the donkey? He knew how to focus.

## THE DONKEY

One day a farmer's donkey fell down into a well. The animal cried piteously for hours as the farmer tried to figure out what to do. Finally, he decided the animal was old, and the well needed to be covered up anyway; it just wasn't worth it to retrieve the donkey.

He invited all his neighbours to come over and help him. They all grabbed a shovel and began to shovel dirt into the well. At first, the donkey realised what was happening and cried horribly. Then to everyone's amazement, he quieted down.

A few shovel loads later, the farmer finally looked down the well. He was astonished at what he saw.

With each shovel of dirt that hit his back, the donkey was doing something amazing. He would shake it off and take a step up. He was making steps.

As the farmer's neighbours continued to shovel dirt on top of the animal, he would shake it off and take a step up. Pretty soon, everyone was amazed as the donkey stepped up over the edge of the well and happily trotted off!

Life is going to shovel dirt on you, all kinds of dirt. The trick to getting out of the well is to shake it off and take a step up. Each of our troubles is a stepping stone. We can get out of the deepest wells just by not stopping, never giving up! Shake it off and take a step up.

*Aim for the top . . . It's too crowded at the bottom.*

Failure and fear go hand in hand. Let's smash these bad boys next.

# 7

# Scared to Fail? Not Anymore!

*You have to lose a few battles to win the war.*

What's wrong with failure? This is an opportunity to begin again more intelligently and better prepared. It's also essential to get acquainted with it because everything you want is on the other side of fear. Failure has been labelled badly because this a great chance to give yourself feedback.

Fear causes worry, which is a total waste of imagination, as Einstein said.

Our deepest fears are like dragons, guarding our deepest treasures.

Fear is a real prison, and the only real freedom is freedom from fear. My grandmother told me that faith can move mountains. I've learnt that my doubts can create them. The world is going to judge you, no matter what you do, so live your life the way you want to.

When everything is going against you, remember that an airplane takes off against the wind, not with it so

> Laugh your heart out.
> Dance in the rain.
> Cherish the moments.
> Ignore the pain.
> Live, love, laugh.
> Forgive and forget.
> Life is too short
> To live with regret.

Great spirits have faced violent opposition from mediocre minds. Yes, some people want you to fail. It rationalises why they are not successful if they see you fail. These are the real failures. They fail once and give up. You don't do that. You are doing this for you, not them. Do not let them take space in your head, unless they are paying you.

I once heard a speaker talk about a failure called 'Tony If Only.' Tony would say, 'If only I did this, if only I did that.' It became his mantra. Don't be 'Tony If Only.' Be 'Sam Who Can' or 'The Kid Who Did.'

It's not usually failure that holds you back. It's the fear of failure that paralyses you, and yet failure is a greater teacher than success. Failing shows you how not to do it so that success becomes easier with every failure. Every winner I have met has overcome his or her fears and worries.

Notice on my wall—PLEASE DO NOT FEED THE FEARS.

It may seem that you are in a dark place when things are not going to plan, but there are always cracks to let the light in.

> *If you set your goals ridiculously high and it's a failure, you will fail above most people's success.*
> —James Cameron

I said earlier that sometimes you find yourself in the middle of nowhere, and sometimes in the middle of nowhere, you find yourself. Somebody very close to me once went to prison. He loved this phrase and took full advantage of it. He used the time to read, get fit and healthy, and focus. He made the best of a bad situation when many others failed, and now he is very successful as an international entrepreneur.

Failure is an opportunity to begin again more intelligently as long as you don't quit because

> When things go wrong as they sometimes will,
> When the road you're trudging seems all up hill;
> When the funds are low and the debts are high,
> And you want to smile, but you have to sigh;
> When care is pressing you down a bit,
> Rest if you must, but don't you quit.
> Life is strange with its twists and turns
> As every one of us sometimes learns.
> And many a failure comes about
> When he might have won had he stuck it out.
> Don't give up, though the pace seems slow—
> You may succeed with another blow.
> Success is failure turned inside out—
> The silver tint of the clouds of doubt.
> And you never can tell just how close you are,

> It may be near when it seems so far.
> So stick to the fight when you're hardest hit— It's
> when things seem worst that you must not quit.
> —'Don't Quit,' John Greenleaf Whittier

Quitters never win, and winners never quit. If you follow the earlier steps, they will remove a lot of the fear, but don't be afraid to fail. Let's clear one thing up: Failure *is* an option. Quitting is *not*.

**Granddad Tip: When you realise that failure is feedback, giving you knowledge and experience, it becomes beneficial. So hurry up and fail some more.**

We know that the strongest hearts have the most scars, and what is more beautiful than a smile shining through the tears of struggle?

You have to take some failure, factor it in to your plan, because if you can't take it, you can't make it.

It's okay to make the mistakes. This is your chance to regroup and recharge, knowing that you are more knowledgeable, and with a few failures behind you, you will be more knowledgeable.

Here's a lovely quotable quote:

> *If you only do things you can do, you will
> never be more than you are.*
> —Kung Fu Panda

And whilst we are in the mood, here are some more from the greats:

> *Failure isn't fatal, but failure to change might be.*
> —John Wooden

*Failure should be our teacher, not our undertaker. Failure is delay, not defeat. It is a temporary detour, not the end. Failure is something we avoid by only by saying nothing, doing nothing, and being nothing.*
—Denis Waitley

*There is no failure except in no longer trying.*
—Chris Bradford

*There is only one thing that makes a dream impossible to achieve: the fear of failure.*
—Paulo Coelho

*Success is stumbling from failure to failure with no loss of enthusiasm.*
—Winston Churchill

*The only real mistake is the one from which we learn nothing.*
—Henry Ford

*Winners are not afraid of losing. But losers are. Failure is part of the process of success. People who avoid failure also avoid success.*
—Robert T Kiyosaki

*It's not how far you fall, but how high you bounce back that counts.*
—Zig Ziglar

*Every adversity, every failure, every heartache carries with it the seed of an equal or greater benefit.*
—Napoleon Hill

*When we give ourselves permission to fail, we at the same time give ourselves permission to excel.*
—Eloise Ristad

*What is the point of being alive if you don't at least try to do something remarkable?*
—John Green

*Failure is so important. We speak about success all the time. It is the ability to resist or use failure that often leads to greater success. I've met people who don't try for the fear of failing.*
—J K Rowling

*We are failures—at least the best of us are.*
—J M Barrie

*Failures are finger posts on the road to achievement.*
—C S Lewis

*If you're not prepared to be wrong, you'll never come up with anything original.*
—Ken Robinson

You have probably heard by now that it took Edison ten thousand attempts to create the light bulb. When he was told he failed ten thousand times, he replied, 'No, I did not. I found ten thousand ways it would not work.'

A big problem is expectations over reality. I'll run with my expectations. People who expect things will release a chemical into their body called endorphins. Athletes know all about this. They expect to win, but in reality, many are aiming for something that has not been achieved yet.

They are breaking records they have never achieved before. Every year, in sport and business, new records are broken. They could not do this if the fears were big. They tame their fears with thought control. David was probably scared when he faced Goliath, but it didn't stop him. So as we said earlier, 'Feel the fear, but do it anyway.'

Michael Jordan was considered one of the greatest sportsmen ever. He was a basketball superstar. Here's his thoughts on his failures and why they contributed to his success:

> I have missed more than nine thousand shots in my career. I have lost almost three hundred games. Twenty-six times, I have been trusted to take the game winning shot and missed. I've failed over and over again in my life, and that's why I succeed.

I have never met a strong person with an easy past.

Sometimes the fear will not go away, so you'll have to do it afraid, but do it, you must, because you won't always succeed, because you are exceptionally talented. You will succeed because you are exceptionally determined.

*Delapsus resurgum—when I fall, I shall rise.*

I believe that your life begins or restarts where fear ends. You have the talent, skills, and ability to succeed. Now do you have the guts to fail?

Treat failure with respect because success has one thousand fathers, whilst failure is a lonely orphan. So don't make yourself lonely.

*The phoenix must burn to rise.*

And keep in mind that neither success nor failure is ever final. You have to keep moving.

> *Named must your fear be, before banish it you can.*
> —Master Yoda, *Star Wars*

**Granddad Tip: If the fear won't go away, tame it.**

A big stumbling block to not dealing with fear and failure is procrastination.

Let's deal with that now . . . . And not put it off.

# 8

# Why Now and Not Tomorrow

*If you really want to do something you will find a way. If you don't you will find an excuse.*
—Jim Rohn

I bought a book once on procrastination, but I haven't got round to reading it yet. It's not funny. That's what this is about. Don't do today what you can put off until tomorrow—that's what many really think.

Slay it now. Putting off a task is more stressful in the end than doing it. And when you finally get around to it, you won't do it as well.

Procrastination has been called the thief of time, and that's exactly what it does. *It steals your time*; time you will never get back, time you could have used to much better effect, dreaming, designing, or planning your future.

*Don't count time, make time count.*
—Jac Ludlow

You have a bit of a battle here. Your mind is trying to protect you from the things you don't like, and we often end up doing things that's stress-relieving instead of goal-achieving.

This is a big decision that you have to put time into. It's like a credit card, a lot of fun until you get the bill, and the bill is high.

So decide—are you going to be a producer (pull and work forward) or a procrastinator (push things off to tomorrow, next week, or maybe never)?

Watch how quickly a bad day becomes a bad week or bad month.

This leads to negative consequences if not dealt with properly.

***Giggle juice: Procrastination can be a good thing. You will always have something to do tomorrow, and you have nothing to do today.***

**The Wicked Sisters**

Procrastination, partnered with her wicked sister complacency, cost me so much. They still haunt me and are the twin destroyers of success.

It's as though one leads to the other. You start putting things off, and then it becomes almost acceptable. Then a bad habit can lead to the other things we spoke of, mental monsters and very bad habits. Why handicap yourself when it's easy to take action? It's just hard to take the first step.

We know that action cures fears. Indecision and postponement fertilise fears. Hesitation only enlarges and magnifies the fears.

**Lost and Found**

> *One twenty-four-hour twenty-four-carat golden day*
> *Each hour studded with sixty diamond minutes*
> *Each minute studded with sixty ruby seconds*
> *But don't bother to look for it*
> *That wonderful day I lost today*

Break it down, break it up. The only way to eat an elephant is in small bites. This gets you going, so never underestimate the power of small steps. They really do start you towards big changes.

> *If not me, who? If not now, when?*
> *If it is to be, it's up to me.*

## Clutter

Another issue with procrastination is the unfinished jobs, lists and projects everywhere. Now it's hard to start. So keep on top of it.

A cluttered desk often leads to a cluttered mind, so declutter yourself for success. Unfinished jobs are everywhere for the procrastinator, makes them feel busy, but in reality, they are busy fools convincing themselves they have lots to do.

> *Declutter yourself for success.*

So start get rid of the clutter. Clutter comes in many forms and brings with it all the distractions to prevent you from taking action. We know about focus now, so let's get rid of the clutter for a clean start. Messy desk, messy life; messy work, messy life; messy head, messy life. This is all baggage that you need to get rid of. And if its baggage from the past, send it right back where it belongs—to the past.

It's hard to focus when your life is full of distractions. This prevents action. Get everything and everyone out of your life that should not be there. You are then free of the distractions and can focus on taking action. A clear head with minimal distractions. You can control or eliminate minimal distractions.

When I lived in Asia, I loved how they studied feng shui. It included an attitude of 'out with the old, in with the new.' Everything was simple and organised. I call this freedom of the brain—free of clutter and ready to go.

The best advice I can give you regarding clutter is deal with it or ditch it. Don't let it accumulate anywhere in your life.

Did you hear about the Wooslam bird?

The Wooslam bird is a bird which when pursued, flies 'around in ever-decreasing circles until it finally disappears up its own fundamental orifice. From which point of vantage, it showers shit and derision upon its baffled pursuers.'

Know anyone like this? That's what we look like when we are cluttered.

If you want to be successful, do not allow yourself the luxury of excuses.

Just as weeds strangle good plants, this will strangle your future.

## The Two Pains

**These pains are *discipline* and *regret*.**

If you do not discipline yourself to clear the clutter and get on with your work and plans, you will have the worst pain, that of regret. It's often too late then as opportunities have been missed because of inaction.

Train your thoughts with new thinking. Be Wonder Woman, not Wander Woman. Think about great questions to ask yourself to get you going, such as

'I wonder how good it would feel today to go to the gym.'

'I wonder how amazing it will feel when I pack my body with great nutrients.'

'I wonder what resources will show up today to that I haven't discovered yet.'

Now look at what you are doing. With these great questions, you are challenging your brain. Your brain likes that. Even though it is trying to protect you, when you get that great organ on side it's your powerhouse, your engine room. It needs fuel, and apart from good nutrition, it needs great thoughts and challengers. Questions are a great way to get your brain going in the right direction. What else stops us?

*Others may point the way, but you must walk the path.*

## Distraction

'Attraction of distraction' is very dangerous when we look for things that are stress-relieving instead of goal-achieving. Stress-relieving things, such as entertainment, release dopamine, a chemical that makes us feel good, into our body. Dopamine is known as the feel-good neurotransmitter, a chemical that ferries information between neurons. The brain releases it when we eat food that we crave or whilst we are being entertained, contributing to feelings of pleasure and satisfaction as part of the reward system. It's the same with social media.

So why wouldn't we want more of this? We do, but we must learn to defer our gratification until the work is done.

What are your distractions? Just because you can have it doesn't make it right. This includes time, your most valuable resource.

The devil isn't always that religious creature. It's that voice inside you that persuades you not to do things.

Another distraction is obsession with others. This will slow you down. You grow fastest when you are not distracted by others.

## Don't-Do List

This could help. When you next start your lists and review your goals, consider a don't-do list, a list next to the things you want to achieve and a reminder of what you should not be doing; for example:

**Don't-Do List - Today**

1. I will not take calls and e-mails until . . .
2. I will not eat anything unhealthy today until I've achieved . . .
3. I will not watch TV until I have accomplished . . .
4. I will not get distracted from my exercise program . . .

So if we can slay this dragon, it's time for action.

Ready to take action?

# 9

# Taking Action

*I love quotes, but in the end, knowledge has to be converted into action or it's worthless.*
—Tony Robbins

Did you wake up today to be mediocre? A warrior is not the one who always wins, but the one who always fights, and we know now that action-takers are the money-makers.

The bridge between where you are and who you want to become is discipline. The biggest weight on that bridge is excuses. Excuses are for people who don't want it bad enough. Be stronger than your excuses.

Things change pretty quickly when you take action, and it's not so bad. I've learnt that what comes easy won't last, and what lasts won't come easy.

Taking action usually means 'change.' Please don't run from change—run to it. We can all improve on the brain we are given. It's designed for that. So strap yourself in and come with me on a journey from your past into your future.

Let's shuffle and shift, hustle and bustle, because taking action is the magic that removes fear. It is the work, and all you have to do now is START.

There's a wonderful feeling that ignites your whole body when you start something and see it grow. Often with small incremental gains, this builds on habits that we discussed earlier. A great habit is the habit of starting. Once you start something, you are committed to some form of progress. When the progress happens, your juices are flowing. This is action in action. Trust your hard work. It's unlocking doors you can't see yet.

Taking action is one source of your happiness.

**Granddad Tip: Once you start seeing the results of self-improvement, it really becomes addictive. You start falling in love with the person you're becoming, the places you're going, the things you're doing, and it motivates you to work even harder with a more focussed energy.**

## Start Small—But Start

> *You don't have to be great to get started, but*
> *you have to get started to be great.*

It doesn't have to start big. Everything you see that is big started small. Yes, small choices make big changes, and small steps create giant leaps.

> *I love the smell of possibility in the morning.*

Light the pilot light of self-development and watch the growth sparks flying in perfect formation. Taking action starts with you. This is another exciting aspect of taking action. I can take you to where winning is made. It's not far, but it will seem way out of your comfort zone TO START WITH. Then it gets easier when it's a routine. This is a great place to be. It's where all the opportunities live. It's the place that takes you to where you do something very new. Yes, to get something we never had, we have to do something we never did. Get comfortable outside your comfort zone. Great things happen there. Great people live there.

How do you find this place? It will find you. The world will not make it easy to get there, but the world will make it easy to find. Yes, it will message you every day. You will hear a whisper every day, saying, 'Give up. You don't need this. It's different here. Don't come.'

Then that little warrior inside says, 'Try once more, just one more time.'

And so often, when your inner warrior shows up, and you listen to her, she brings the keys to open up everything outside of your comfort zone. She is the star of this chapter. Please get to know her well. She will appear first in thoughts, she then shows up in your plan, and she comes alive when you take action.

Taking action gets you out of your comfort zone (or danger zone) fast. Now you are learning, learning what to do and what not to do. Yes, we need to fail sometimes, and this is where it happens. This is where we get the building blocks of success serving us.

Successful people do what needs to be done, when it needs to be done, whether they feel like it or not. Please read that again.

Some enjoy the self-pity of being one of life's doormats. The medicine is action.

At some point, you have to either shit or get off the pot.

Getting started is a form of active inspiration that naturally produces momentum. Then motivation kicks in. After that, it's not 'What am I going to do?' It's 'What am I going to do next or now?' Here's the momentum coming again.

Sir Isaac Newton taught us that objects in motion stay in motion, so let's move, move forward, and keep moving.

There's a difference between *motivation* and *inspiration*.

> *Motivation is when you get hold of an idea and carry it through to its conclusion, and inspiration is when an idea gets hold of you and carries you where you are intended to go.*
> —Dr Wayne Dyer

Motivation is an inside job. Inspiration soon evaporates. Let me explain. Have you watched a movie or listened to a great speaker who inspired you? It feels great for about twenty minutes after the event. Then it's gone.

I once read from a fortune cookie that many a false step was taken by standing still.

> *You can read all the books you like on riding a bike, but until you get on the bike and try it, you have no idea.*
> —Nate Tillery

Same with life.

Do it now because NOW is what you have. Now is what you can control. Now is a great resource, which, if you get rid of the clutter and distractions, will be the start of your new future. It's starts NOW.

> *Yesterday is history.*
> *Tomorrows a mystery.*
> *Today is the present.*
> *And that's why they call it a gift.*

**Remember DIN**

**D** o
**I** t
**N** ow.

You will get an amazing rush of confidence when you keep the promises you made to yourself.

Here's a little tip to help you find the time. Make it a priority, and the time will show up.

*It's always the start that requires the greatest effort.*

## Manage Your Expectations

Nothing works the first time. If you don't take action, nothing will happen. You will not have the habit. Then you become satisfied. Then you take the opportunities you don't want. Then you get comfortable with lower standards. That's the shortcut to the 'danger zone.' You are better than this. Don't fall for it.

Success and failure are engineered by actions or inactions, with very few exceptions.

Here is an action to consider. Find your passion and figure out how to get paid for it. Imagine the energy you will apply to something that you are passionate about, like getting paid for something you love doing. How could you not be great at doing something you love and improving every day? This is not just action, but inspired action. Inspiration is contagious in a productive way, so others benefit also. There are many others who like the things you love. Help them get close to it, and make it your business, full or part time.

Get your ideas in action. I've lost count of how many times I've heard people say that's a stupid idea, but when someone took action on it, it became a success. Here are a few examples. Imagine if you were an investor and somebody pitched these ideas to you.

1. **Teenage Mutant Ninja Turtles**

Four mutant turtle characters named after Renaissance painters. Their boss is a rat. They eat nothing but pizza and fight crime from the sewers in New York. Are you in?

Hasbro toys, the no. 1 toy manufacturer in America in the '80s rejected this. Yet they became the biggest toy seller at the time. They continued to make movies and sell merchandise on a massive scale.

## 2. Facebook

The world needs yet another social network *a la* Myspace or Friendster, except several years late. We'll only open it up to a few thousand overworked, antisocial Ivy Leaguers. Everyone else will then follow since Harvard students are so cool.

## 3. Dropbox

We built a file-sharing and syncing solution in a market that has a dozen of them built by big companies like Microsoft. It has only one feature, and you have to move all your content to use it.

Who would fall for this?

## 4. Amazon

We'll sell books online, even though users are still scared to use credit cards on the Web. Their shipping costs will eat up any money they save. They'll do it for the convenience, even though they have to wait a week for the book.

This created one of the richest men in the world.

## 5. Virgin Atlantic

Airlines are fun, so we are starting one. How hard could it be? We'll differentiate with a funny safety video and by not being a–holes.

Now a great well-respected airline from a guy who started selling secondhand books and records in a market stall.

### 6. Craigslist

They said it will be ugly. It will be free. Except for the scammers and hookers. Now a huge business.

### 7. iOS

We are shipping a brand-new operating system that doesn't run a single one of the millions of applications that have already been developed for Mac OS, Windows, and Linux. Apple has to approve all the apps, and it won't have cut and paste to start with.

### 8. Google

We are building the world's twentieth search engine at a time when most of the others have been abandoned as commoditised money losers. We'll strip out all the ad-supported news and portal features so you won't be distracted from using the free search stuff.

### 9. PayPal

People will use their unsecure AOL and Yahoo e-mail addresses to pay one another real money, backed by a non-bank with a cute name run by twenty-somethings.

Now the international standard for payment.

### 10. Instagram

Who needs Facebook? We got filters! That's right, filters! This got so big that Facebook bought them.

## 11. LinkedIn

How about a professional social network aimed at busy thirty- and forty-somethings? They will use it once every five years when they go job searching.

Millions and millions of users and now the biggest business networking site in history.

## 12. Tesla

Instead of just building batteries and selling them to Detroit, we are going to build our own cars from scratch plus own the distribution network. We'll start the company during a recession and the crashing of the clean tech industry.

From the inventor of PayPal.

## 13. SpaceX

If NASA can do it, so can we! It isn't rocket science. Oh, it is. Also from the inventor of PayPal.

## 14. Firefox

We are going to build a better Web browser, even though 90 percent of the world's computers already have a free one built in. It's based on a product that a single college student built.

## 15. Twitter

It is like e-mail, SMS, or RSS. Except it only has 140 characters, doesn't support images, can't be made private, and will be used mostly by geeks at first, followed by Britney Spears and Charlie Sheen.

There are so many more examples of what others thought were stupid ideas. A focussed creative mind that takes action will see opportunity, not stupidity.

## The Ivy Lee Method

Here's a one-hundred-year-old strategy that will help you take action and become more productive.

The Ivy Lee method dates back to 1918, when Lee, a productivity consultant, was hired by Charles M. Schwab, the president of the Bethlehem Steel Corporation, to improve his company's efficiency. As the story goes, Lee offered his method to Schwab for free, and after three months, Schwab was so pleased with the results he wrote Lee a check for $25,000—the equivalent of about $400,000 today.

**How does it work?**

- Under the Ivy Lee method, at the end of each night, you write down your six most important tasks to accomplish the following day in order of importance.
- The next day, you begin working on the tasks one at a time.
- The strategy works because it reduces 'decision fatigue,' saves you time, and forces you to prioritise your goals.

|   | Tasks – Top 6 | Completed |
|---|---|---|
| 1 | | |
| 2 | | |
| 3 | | |
| 4 | | |
| 5 | | |
| 6 | | |

This optimises your schedule, which is important for making the most out of every workday. So simple, so effective, and forces you to make decisions.

What are you waiting for? Start this now. **DIN.**

**What else is good about taking action?**

Taking action will bring all sorts of attraction. Others will notice. There's a saying that if you want to get something done, you give it to a busy person. Busy people get things done and are noticed for it. They attract opportunities largely because of their momentum. Attraction requires action.

Remember, it's not volume, it's value. You do not have to do many things. It's the value of what you do that counts, not how much you do. Don't become that busy fool with a head and list full of tasks lulling you into a false sense of security.

The most effective way to do it is to do it and go beyond your dreams. make it intentions.

Let's go to the country for a few minutes. Look at the beauty—the trees, wildflowers, grass, streams, and waterfalls. When that water flows, it's fresh, it looks clear. At the bottom of the waterfall is where all the big fish live, healthy and happy in clean running water.

Now compare that with the stagnant pond. The stench, dead plants and animals—nothing wants to live there. It's all decay or decaying. Now take that same water and put it through a waterwheel and life starts again. It's the movement, it's the momentum, it's the action.

Running water doesn't go stale. Don't be a stagnant pond, and if you are, regenerate by getting going.

I mentioned failure earlier, and that causes disappointment. Disappointment is okay. It shows you have feelings, but you must learn to discipline your disappointment.

This is what the majority are not doing.

This is your shortcut to winning. Winners focus on winning, losers focus on winners, so roll your sleeves up and get in there with them.

The past is where you learnt, the future is where you apply the lessons, don't give up in the middle.

There's a lovely story of a man who showed creative action in prison. I like this.

An old farmer wrote to his rebel son in prison, 'This year I won't be able to plant potatoes because I can't dig the ground. I know if you were here, you would help me.'

His son replied, 'Dad, don't think of digging the ground because that's where I buried the guns.'

The police read the letter, and the very next day the whole ground was dug by police, and they found nothing.

The next day the son wrote again, 'Now go plant your potatoes, Dad. It's the best I can do from here.'

## Efficient versus Effective

Efficiency is the time it takes to complete a project. An efficient person will finish tasks in the shortest amount of time possible, using the least amount of resources. Inefficient people will do the opposite. For example, you may want to communicate more efficiently by using e-mail rather than handwriting notes. Efficiency increases productivity and saves both time and money.

Effectiveness is the level of results achieved. When you are effective, you will produce high-quality results. For example, your work in sales will only be effective if leads are consistently created and followed up. If you are ineffective, you will struggle to persuade customers to buy anything. Your effectiveness has an enormous impact on the quality of a product or service.

Are you going to be efficient or effective?

You can be efficient and look organised and busy, but are you effective?

## My Warrior Program

This was something I designed to help me focus. I had experience and knowledge all over the place. My Warrior Program helped me pull it together. I wanted a quick reference of my goals and objectives supported by experiences and a plan of action. This is not my business plan. It focuses on development and the skills and abilities I need. This, along with my vision board, gives me a quick visual reference to everything I want.

Here's what it included:

1. **Summary of what I want to achieve**

A quick reference to be read regularly

2. **Why I want to achieve it**

This is so important. What does this mean to me?

3. **Current skill set**

List of relevant skills and capabilities, including my skills and capabilities gap.

4. **Previous relevant experiences**

Helps remind me that I have done some of this before

5. **Previous relevant successes**

Proof that I can do this

6. **Breakdown of the goals**

Includes a plan to gain new capabilities and skills

7. **What's in my way?**

The obstacles I need to remove that are blocking the achievement of my goals

8. **Obstacle removal plan**

The action plan to remove the obstacles. With the obstacles removed, there's nothing in my way.

9. **Inspirational quotations**

My favourite quotes to inspire me

10. **Conclusion**

**What else?**

Get in this fight and don't worry about the opposition. 'It's not the size of the dog in the fight, it's the size of the fight in the dog.' You can punch above your weight. Try it.

You will see opportunities that you will think are luck. Luck is where preparation meets opportunity.

Motivation alone is not enough; you must be driven. If you want more inspiration, go back to your vision board and the chapter on 'Dreams and Vision.' That should get you started.

*Screw it, let's do it.*
—Richard Branson

Taking action's best friend is commitment, time to meet her . . .

# 10

# Get Some Skin in the Game

*When you were learning to walk and fell down fifty times, you never once said, 'Maybe this is not for me.'*

You don't have to be the best, but you have to be your best. Very few achieve anything like their best because they don't believe how good they can be. The only limit to your impact on life is your imagination and commitment.

It's time to throw yourself in the deep end. You can't be a little bit pregnant. This is so important. There's a story of the barnyard animals. They all got together and decided that as the farmer was so good to them that they would ensure he would get his favourite meal (breakfast) free for the rest of his life—bacon and eggs in abundance.

All agreed this would be a good idea and should start straight away.

The chicken showed up enthusiastically with some nice large brown fresh eggs. The farmer would love these. 'Where's Porky?'

they all said, looking for the pig. After a while, they found him cowering in the haystack, hiding and scared. 'Come on, Porky!' they all shouted. 'A deal is a deal.'

To which Porky responded, 'It's all right for you guys, you're only participating, I'm involved.'

Wow, that's powerful. Are you just participating, or are you involved? Something to think about.

Commitment involves dedication, an obligation to commit to something, so make it worthwhile to you.

And be your best because

The contest lasted moments
Though the training's taken years
But it wasn't the winning alone
That was worth the work and tears.
The applause will be forgotten
That prize will be replaced
But those long hard hours of practise
Will never be a waste
For in trying to win you develop a skill
You learn that winning depends on will
But you cannot grow by how much you win
You only grow by how much you put in
So in this new adventure
That you have begun
Give it your best
AND YOU'VE ALREADY WON

You don't have to be perfect. Perfection kills creativity. Be persistent because when all else fails, persistency prevails.

Your promises will not make you a better person, your commitment will. So fall in love with the process of what you do, and the results will take care of themselves.

If you expect great things from yourself, you will move towards the environment and the resources to achieve more.

No one rises to lower expectations, so in your commitment, keep expectations high.

**Giggle juice: Whatever you do, always give 100 percent, unless you're giving blood.**

Who is the person responsible for **your:**

| | | |
|---|---|---|
| Outlook | | Happiness |
| | Decisions | |
| Actions | | Responses |
| | Attitude | |
| Future | | Thoughts |
| | Behavior | |
| Reputation | | Words |
| | Progress | |
| Influence | | Grades |
| | Accomplishments | |
| Appearance | | Choices |

**You can find her in ….the mirror.**

# 11
# Keep the Confidence, Ditch the Ego

*Egos, egos everywhere*
*They damage and they strain*
*So pick these little monsters up*
*And ditch them in the drain*

*Ego* is the Latin word for 'I.' So if a person seems to begin every sentence with 'I,' it's sometimes a sign of a big ego. We would generally use ego simply to mean our sense of self-worth, whether exaggerated or not. When used in the 'exaggerated' sense, ego is almost the same thing as conceit. Meeting a superstar athlete without a trace of this kind of ego would be a most refreshing experience. But having a reasonable sense of your own worth is no sin. Life's little everyday victories are good, in fact, necessary, for a healthy ego.

So used properly, your ego is good for you, but it must be tamed.

It's a nice temporary feeling that we all enjoy but can be dangerous. Many won't like people with a big ego; some will be envious or, worse still, jealous. It's a temporary fix and should be treated as such.

It can work the other way too. Sometimes, when you feel like you are not enough, you chase external validation. Do you want others to massage your ego? There's no need, you are enough.

Your ego will give you a sense of self-esteem or self-importance. It will appear loud, but it's not the volume, it's the value that matters.

Many people with big egos want to be right all the time. What's more important—being right or having the right results?

Don't tell them how good you are. Let them catch you at it. This is the wow factor when they are not expecting it. If you keep telling them how good you are, they might be disappointed, but if they see you in action and are not expecting it . . . Many great things were accomplished before we were born.

*Climb the mountain so you can see the world, not so the world can see you.*

Enjoy the short-term rush of approval, acceptance, acknowledgement, then move on with humility. Being humble is not thinking less of yourself. It's thinking of yourself less.

A healthy ego is good and will build you and others who admire you. An unhealthy ego will appear as conceit and will not help you. Go for respect, not attention. It lasts longer.

Many well-educated people have small egos. Maybe knowledge gives us a good substitute.

> *Check your ego at the door. The ego can be the great success inhibitor. It can kill opportunities, and it can kill success.*
> —Dwayne Johnson

Sacrifice popularity and ego for amazing results, and when you are wrong, admit it. No one ever choked by swallowing their pride. Do you want respect or attention?

**Granddad Tip: We are not the chosen few, but we can be the few who have chosen.**

Do you want titles or testimonies? People who shine from within do not need the spotlight. Be careful when someone tries to trigger you by insulting you or by saying something that annoys you. Slow down and breathe. Switch your ego off. Remember that if you are easily offended, you will be *easily manipulated*.

Ready to change?

# 12

## Could You Change?

*When you change the way you look at things,
the things you look at change.*

Change is not a threat to your life. So many are resistant to change. Treat it as an invitation to live, an improvement to your life, to grow, to enhance, to improve. You still have all your experiences, nobody can take them, but at different times in your life, you will need to change.

I think the main reason people are resistant to change is that they focus on what they have to give up instead of what they have to gain.

Our lives do not get better by chance. We get better by change. If you are not ready for change, try to change the way you look at things. This is a great start.

Here's an example. Read the following, and tell me what you read.

## OPPORTUNITYISNOWHERE.

What do you see? Most tell me they see OPPORTUNITY IS NOWHERE. But if you look at the exact same words without changing them, you could see OPPORTUNITY IS NOW HERE.

Here's another example. Read the following, and tell me what you read.

**Finished files are the result of years of scientific study combined with the experience of many years.**

Now count how many Fs you saw? Done it? How many did you get? Most get three. Here they are in CAPs so that you easily see them.

**Finished (1) Files (2) are the result of years of scientiFic (3) study combined with the experience of many years.**

Did you get them? What about the other three? Let's dig deeper. Here's the other three in CAPs.

**Finished files are the result oF (1) years oF (2) scientific study combined with the experience oF (3) many years.**

Why do so many people miss this? Our mind tricked us to read the F instead of as a V, and we were not looking for the V. We were looking for the F.

Do you think our mind could be tricking us elsewhere? Progress is not automatic, but change is, so embrace it. Another reason to embrace change is that change will not ask for permission. Change just happens, so be prepared as best you can.

One thing you will enjoy is seeing the change in you. Yes, you change many times throughout your life. Your vision and goals will help you change into a better person. Anthony de Mallo said,

> *To a disciple who was forever complaining*
> *about others, the Master said,*
> *'If it is peace you want, seek to change yourself, not*
> *other people. It is easier to protect your feet with*
> *slippers than to carpet the whole of the earth.'*

**Granddad Tip: Don't be afraid to start all over again. This time you are not starting from scratch, you are starting from experience. Whatever you are not changing, you are choosing. Read that again.**

> *Change doesn't always mean getting better, but*
> *getting better always involves change.*

If you can change, or change the way you look at things, you are ready for learning and education.

# 13

# Learning and Education

*The people who are crazy enough to think they can change the world, are the ones that do.*
—Steve Jobs

In school, the role of your teacher is to give you information and knowledge. He or she has all the knowledge you need until you leave school, and it's your job to make the transfer. So soak up that knowledge whenever you can and store it in your brain to call on when you need it.

There's a big difference between 'skill set' and 'mind set.' Some people have a natural skill to learn quickly and store knowledge. Others have to work at it *initially*. After a while, it becomes a habit, and then it's easier, and we know from a previous chapter how important and powerful habits are.

The school process is a process of repetition and reinforcement. It's sometimes boring just learning facts and detail. School will condition you to obey, copy, memorise, and conform.

In school, your mind is like a suitcase that gets filled for sixteen years.

Add stories and drama by asking more about what's behind the lesson. Ask how you can apply this knowledge, what's in it for you. Then it becomes more valuable.

Your mind is like a parachute, it works best when it's open. So keep an open inquisitive mind and question everything.

There is beauty, benefit, and battle in learning. A few battles are healthy. They prepare you in other ways for other experiences. Get into battle early to benefit from the beauty of learning.

**Granddad Tip: Do it quicker than the others. The faster you learn, the faster you earn.**

## Questions

There is a magic in questions. When you ask questions, your mind is seeking answers at the start. It's exploring. This is a great time to learn, and don't forget, they are your questions.

Short questions usually get long answers, and long questions usually get short answers. For example, if I ask you, 'What was special about coming to school today?' That's a long question and will force you to think and describe and will usually get a short answer.

If you tell me, you had a special journey to school today, and I simply ask 'Why?' or 'How?' you will go into detail to describe why.

Use your six friends to help you with your question technique.

> I have six friends.
> I know them well,
> Called who, what, why,
> Where, how, and when.

My favourite question for you is, instead of what do you want to be when you grow up, think about what problems you want to solve. This changes the conversation from 'who do I want to work for' to 'what do I need to learn to be able to do that.'

Get good at maths so that people don't cheat you. Learn geometry by shooting pool. *The angle of incidence is equal to the angle of reflection.* Be unconventional if it helps you learn. It's not always about formal education. It's often about being in the right environment, being around the right people, people who want to learn, improve, and share. If you're the smartest person in the room, you are in the wrong room.

Sharing knowledge with the right people spreads quickly with enthusiasm. It's enlightening and stimulating. It's good to help others learn but only if they want to. Never try to teach a pig to sing. You'll be wasting your time, and you'll annoy the pig.

*Smart people learn from everything and everyone, average people from their experiences, stupid people already have all the answers.*
—Socrates

## Getting to Know Yourself—Great Questions to Ask Yourself

There is a difference between knowing the path and walking the path. Ask yourself these questions and be prepared to learn all about you.

What bugs you and why?

How old will you be when you learn your second language?

What will you be the first at?

How many things are you in the top 10 of?

Who has you helped the most and how did it feel?

Do you want what's best or what's best for you?

Are you focussing on what you are doing or what you are becoming?

Are you forcing yourself into doing things or are you committed?

Are you achieving to be happy or happily achieving?

What makes you happy?

What do you like daydreaming about?

If you could do anything right now, what would you do?

What makes you feel brave?

What does it feel like when you hug someone you love?

What makes you feel loved?

Who makes you feel loved and why?

How would you design your tree house?

What do you enjoy giving?

If you could give £100 to charity, who would it be and why?

If you designed clothes what would they look like?

What will you dream about tonight?

How do you best like helping others?

What makes you feel thankful?

What makes you feel energised?

If you were a photographer for the day, what would you take pictures of?

What would be your great day?

What makes you awesome?

What are the three things you want to do this winter?

If you could make up a new holiday, what would it look like?

What projects give you energy? What projects drain you?

Which people give you energy? Which people drain you?

I defy you to ask yourself these questions. Answer them and be bored.

A beautiful thing about learning is that no one can take it away from you. But remember, school rewards fast learners, life rewards deep learners.

**It's Not Just the Classroom**

If you are willing to learn, no one can stop you. If you are not, no one can help you.

Learning and education in your life is what sharpening an axe is to woodcutting. Are you green and growing or ripe and rotten?

Treat your whole life as a continuous university. All the subjects are connected. All the sciences are related. Languages are beautiful with different tones and gestures. Learn the structure, and boss English. This is your mother tongue and widely spoken in the world. The English language is like a giant sponge, but it has lots of holes. Learn the beautiful words because they open doors, give you esteem and understanding. They will improve your circles of influence.

You need the expertise that gives you credibility and allows you to tap into your passion. You have to learn and experience this.

You have the power to change things with words. Words give you more access to more people and more opportunities. Get in more people's lives and brains.

> *The best teacher is experience—it gives*
> *you the test first then the lesson.*
> —Oscar Wilde

Learning and education will give you influence. Influence will give you affluence.

> *Life is a succession of lessons that have to be lived to be understood.*
> —Ralph Emerson

Your PC, phone, or other devices are like an ATM of knowledge. Teach yourself—yes, DIY learning and education. It's never been easier with interactive programs and lessons to learn and keep up to date. We must keep up to date and use our knowledge and education. Use it or lose it.

To help with a shortcut to memory retention, consider mind maps and memory trees. These are a great way to recall information using diagrams that are written in a way your brain thinks and can follow easy.

You don't need to be perfect, just make regular progress. Progress beats perfection. Show me where perfection lives, and I'll move there.

Why not take this further and help others? The biggest beneficiary of training and teaching is often the teacher. This is repetition and reinforcement at its best.

Most are in the rat race. They get up in the morning, go to work, come home, watch TV, go to bed. Next day, get up go to work, come home, watch TV, go to bed. They do this for seventy-five years and die. They then wonder what happened?

Learning takes a bit of work and the magic that removes the fear is the work. This will get you out of the rat race because the winner of the rat race is still a rat.

Leaders are readers. This is so important. All the great leaders I can think of are or were avid readers. There's a connection with a book that I believe is more personal than other forms of learning. You and you alone are determining how you interpret the book and what the words mean to you.

**Granddad Tip: Design your daily playlist, and I don't mean music.**

I hope books are still in vogue and not just digital when you read this. There's a different connection with a book. You highlight things and scribble in your own handwriting. Writing things down crystallises your thoughts. Reading is to your mind what exercise is to your body. I love being between the pages of a book. It's a great place to be.

> *Learn the rules like a pro so that you can break them like an artist.*
> —Picasso

And finally, on learning and education, *always know more than you show, and always say less than you know.*

What's the difference between intelligence and wisdom?

# 14

# Intelligence versus Wisdom: It's Your Call

*I grabbed my book, and it opened up my soul.*

I have no personal comment to make on this section. This is where you ponder.

There are profound distinctions between *intelligence* and *wisdom*. Explore them.

Intelligence can lead to arguments. Wisdom leads to settlements.

Intelligence is power of will. Wisdom is power *over* will.

Intelligence is heat; it burns. Wisdom is warmth; it comforts.

Intelligence is pursuit of knowledge; it tires the seeker. Wisdom is pursuit of truth; it inspires the seeker.

Intelligence is holding on. Wisdom is letting go.

Intelligence leads you. Wisdom guides you.

An intelligent man understands what is being said; a wise man, what is left unsaid.

An intelligent man speaks when he has to say something; a wise man speaks when he has something to say.

An intelligent man sees everything as relative; a wise man sees everything as related.

An intelligent man tries to control the mass flow; a wise man navigates the mass flow.

An intelligent man preaches; a wise man teaches.

Intelligence is good, but wisdom achieves great results.

> *A smart person knows what to say; a wise person knows whether to say it or not.*
> —Dalai Lama

**Seven Lovely Logic**

1. Make peace with your past so it doesn't spoil your present.
2. What others think of you is none of your business.
3. Time heals almost everything. Give time some time.
4. No one is the reason for your happiness except yourself.
5. Don't compare your life to others. You have no idea what their journey is all about.
6. Stop thinking too much. It's all right not to know all the answers.
7. Smile. You don't own all the problems in the world.

*Grades don't measure intelligence, and age doesn't define maturity.*

Next, I want to talk about family and friends—yours.

# 15

# Family and Friends

*Families are like branches on a tree. We all go in different directions, but our roots remain the same.*

Family is important because it provides love, support, and a framework of values to each of its members. Family members teach one another, serve one another, and share life's joys and sorrows. Families provide a setting for your personal growth. Your family is the single most important influence in your life.

**Your family will . . .**

- Give you utmost protection
- Give you security
- Shape your future
- Be your first school
- Shape your character
- Set rules and values
- Discipline you
- Prepare you for the world

- Provide a safe sanctuary to return to whenever you need them
- Be your first medics
- Give you knowledge
- Give you your first real love
- Give you a genuine sense of belonging

It's hard to appreciate fully your parents until you become one, and here are my thoughts on your parents:

You're surrounded by two angels
And not the ones above
But those right here and there for you
A very special love
They will expect a lot from you
Things that are a must
They bring a special magic
A bit like fairy dust

They are there for you whenever
If you're happy or you're sad
They will always be your first love
Your special Mum and Dad
In the rain, they will find you rainbows
In the dark, they will find you stars
When you're sad, they'll make you happy
So you don't carry the scars
You can have a step-mummy or daddy
That's not wrong or bad
You can have as many as you like
But there's only *one* Mum and Dad

One thing I did every year was to send a New Year's message. We have a Facebook Messenger group that includes your mum and dad, Nanny, Uncle Jac, and Lidia. I wanted a positive reflection on the previous year and some encouragement and inspiration for the coming year.

**Here's my actual message for 2021:**

*Last year, I started my message by saying that 2020 will be a challenging year. I had no idea what was coming. Let's reflect.*

*Despite a global pandemic, a world depression, and an economic meltdown, we have all once again grown.*

*Just imagine what we can achieve in the good times. We did it, we do it, again and again and again.*

*Every year in my message, it's getting easier to present positive news from our close circle.*

*Please keep this family tradition of NYD message going long after me. It's easy to forget our achievements, and this is a lovely way to reflect. And it won't be long before we read this with our princesses.*

*As a proud self-appointed head of this family, I am moved to remind you of a quote from the* Jungle Book, *albeit one that you have heard before.*

*Rudyard Kipling, the author of the* Jungle Book, *was a genius to come up with a story of a young boy who finds himself lost in a jungle, surrounded by danger, fear, and dangerous animals. Anything familiar there? Sounds just like life. Mowgli stayed strong and survived. He mixed with the right creatures and followed the rules of the jungle. You may think the quote is 'Sometimes you find yourself in the middle of nowhere, and sometimes in the middle of nowhere, you find yourself.'* But that's not the quote I want to share with you. When it really mattered and we needed help, we got it all from within our family.

*In my darkest moments, I took great comfort knowing I had the best support group flowing through my veins from my family and with open arms, from my daughters-in-law. I know from the bottom of my heart that my grandchildren can tap into that whenever they need help, support, or love.*

*The quote I'm referring to is a favourite that I have used before. I want to remind you that*

> The strength of the wolf is in the pack . . . And
> the strength of the pack is in the wolf.

*I am proud to see how all our adult wolves have grown to protect and support, and how great is it to see our strong young cubs growing and developing—our pack!*

*They will be ready to go into their jungle and will be fully prepared to survive and thrive.*

**Poet's Corner**

*My feet are blistered, my fingers tingle.*
*There was only one place I wanted to mingle.*
*You can keep the booze, the drugs, and the crack.*
*When the chips are down, I got my pack.*

*In business and personal development, you are creating your future. That excites the hell out of me.*

*Does that make us the chosen few? No, we are the few who have chosen. We all run our own businesses, and none of us have jobs. We chose to take the risk. We chose to take control of our lives and futures.*

*So what about the pack? Jac's new biz is looking good, diversifying into new ventures and jumping in at the bottom of something he had no knowledge of.*

*He has three brands now and proved he can diversify, and the product is irrelevant when you understand business. Our Jockey boy created a new stronger future.*

*Dee, consolidating everything and learning from great experiences, is a brand now, and nothing can or will stop him. He has mastered the most powerful communication tool—social media. In such a short period, he made great connections and impressed the business community. Who would have thought ten years ago that the three of us would be applauded by a great bunch of entrepreneurs, delivering valuable talks? We all had great feedback from a forum created by my son—The 5AM Club.*

*Lidia, my lil pixie, as professional and consistent as ever, building on the foundations she laid and now a gourmet chef to challenge us. It was lovely sharing your ideas and feeding off your enthusiasm. And the big event is finally planned for this year!*

*Mick's coming through the toughest year in her career. Mick and Lid are dependent on seeing clients in person. The rest of us can get by remotely. I bet Mick spent a lot of that time developing and bonding with our girls. I love to see them with her and her with them.*

*As for me, I'm so lucky. I have my pack, some great friends, and an amazing health system here in Hong Kong. Last year, I forged some great new business relationships, and I'm as motivated as ever. It's easier for me to be strong knowing you are there.*

*I finally finished my book, passed more heavy exams, and closed the biggest deal of my career. 2021 is calling me for bigger and better things, and I'm ready to answer.*

*When some went to sleep to see their dreams, we stayed awake to work on ours. Please remember this in years to come.*

> *We are Ludlows,*
> *A badge I'm proud to wear.*
> *We can live, love, grow*
> *Almost anywhere.*
> *And when we feel like giving up*
> *Or think we're losing traction,*
> *We kick ourselves right up the butt*
> *And spring back into action.*
> *We study, learn, work very hard,*
> *A trait that everyone knows.*
> *We do it because it's in our blood,*
> *Nine very proud Ludlows.*

*A lot of people know what giving up feels like. We can show 'em what happens when we don't. We could've, so many times, but we didn't.*

*Not just a brand now but an amazing bond.*

*Although the guys in the family are outgunned by girl power, I support of great women behind us is immense.*

*Shara must be run ragged. It's hard work keeping three little munchkins fed, entertained, and always dressed so lovely, even at* home. We all know the effort that takes. Even though you have a great brain for work and business, your calling is elsewhere for now, doing the things you shine at.

Ours girls sparkle individually, but together, they shine.

Sky is a young lady now. I see a grace in her not often found in young ladies.

Chanel has a blend of a funny little munchkin with the ability to do what she wants.

Tienna reminded me that babies are on loan. We don't have them for long. The years fly by.

It won't be long before you are reading our NYD messages.

I wish you great health and strength for the 2021 Jungle. Let's make it look like a walk in the park. I am proud of all of you and could not love you more.

Happy New Year from Papa Wolf, Howlllllllllll xx

*Families that play together, stay together.*

\*\*\*

*Give the ones you love wings to fly, roots to come back, and a reason to stay.*
—Dalai Lama

## Friends

A true friend will last your lifetime; someone usually on your wavelength who will be there in addition to your family, someone to laugh and cry with, whom you can trust with information and secrets. They will want you to succeed with everything you do, rooting for you when things are going your way and supporting you when they are not. Make sure you find and keep many and treat them as gold dust.

The wrong friends are dangerous and can easily influence you into trouble. I'm sure you can suss them out for yourself, but do not underestimate the danger of being with the wrong people and the wrong crowd.

### A Friend Is a Treasure

> A friend is someone to turn to
> When our spirits need a lift.
> A friend is someone we treasure
> Because true friendship is a gift.
> A friend is someone we laugh with
> Over little personal things.
> A friend is someone we're serious with
> In facing whatever life brings.
> A friend is someone who fills our lives
> With beauty, joy, and grace
> And makes the world we live in
> A better, happier place.

*I have learnt that it is not what I've got in life, it's who I got in life.*

We all want a little bit of happiness.

# 16

# Happiness

*Embrace the glorious mess that you are.*

If it's about happiness, stop pushing too hard on the door called happiness. It opens inward.

The Dalai Lama said, 'The key to life is happiness.' That's how important he thought this is. Something this important needs some time. But whose responsibility is it? I'm sure you know by now. No one can make you happy. You have to agree and sign it off. It's your job to make you happy.

Sometimes it's not about what you add to your life. To be happy, many people need to remove things from their life like baggage or anchors weighing you down and holding you back.

**Here are fifteen things to get rid of that I believe will make you happier.**

1. **Give up the need to always be right.**

*Would I rather be right, or would I rather be kind?*
—Wayne Dyer

2. **Give up your need for control.**

   *By letting it go, it all gets done. The world is won by those who let go. When you try and try, the world is beyond winning.*
   —Lao Tzu

3. **Give up on blaming others.**

   *A man can fall many times, but he isn't a failure until he begins to blame somebody else.*
   —John Burroughs

4. **Give up on self-defeating self-talk.**

   *The mind is a superb instrument if it's used correctly. Used wrongly, however, it becomes very destructive.*
   —Eckhart Tolle

5. **Give up on limiting beliefs.**

   *A belief is not an idea held by the mind. It is an idea that holds the mind.*
   —Elly Roselle

6. **Give up complaining.**

   *You can complain because roses have thorns, or you can rejoice because thorns have roses.*
   —Ziggy

7. **Give up the luxury of criticism.**

   *Spend so much time improving yourself that you have no time left to criticize others.*
   —Christian D Larsen

8. **Give up on your need to impress others.**

   *Don't try to impress others, let them have the fun of trying to impress you.*
   —James R Fisher Jr.

9. **Give up your resistance to change.**

   *Follow your bliss and the universe will open windows where there were only doors.*
   —Joseph Campbell

10. **Give up labels.**

    *The highest form of ignorance is when you reject something you don't know anything about.*
    —Wayne Dyer

11. **Give up on your fears.**

    *The only thing we have to fear is fear itself.*
    —Franklin D Roosevelt

12. **Give up on your excuses.**

    *99% of failures come from people who have the habit of making excuses.*
    —George Washington Carver

13. **Give up the past.**

> *Forget the mistakes of the past and move on to the achievements of the future.*
> —Christian D Larsen

14. **Give up the attachment.**

> *The wise individual doesn't get too attached to any of life's pleasures, knowing that wonderful science is hard at work proving it's bad for him.*
> —Bill Vaughan

15. **Give up living your life to other people's expectations.**

> *The world is a mirror and reflects back your expectations. What you get is what you see. You create your own reality.*
> —Denis Waitley

If you can let the baggage of the past go back where it belongs, you have lightened the load considerably. When you are lighter go fly, it's a nicer journey.

You will meet people who have everything yet are unhappy. Conversely, you will meet people who have nothing but are happy. So instead of achieving to be happy, why not be happily achieving?

It's a choice or state of mind that you can control.

*Giggle juice:*

> **Today you are you. That is truer than true. There is no one alive that is youer than you.**
> —*Dr Seuss*

One of the richest men in my era was Steve Jobs. He was a genius that failed a few times but resilient in his belief. He died very rich. To get there, he gave up much. Here are his wise words on happiness:

**Steve Jobs on Happiness**

Steve Jobs dies a billionaire, with a fortune of $7 billion, at the age of fifty-six, from pancreatic cancer. His last words were reported as

> In other eyes, my life is the essence of success, but aside from work, I have a little joy. And in the end, wealth is just a fact of life to which I am accustomed.
>
> At this moment, lying on the bed, sick and remembering all my life, I realize that all my recognition and wealth that I have is meaningless in the face of imminent death. You can hire someone to drive a car for you, make money for you, but you cannot rent someone to carry the disease for you. One can find material things, but there is one thing that cannot be found when it is lost—LIFE.
>
> Treat yourself well and cherish others. As we get older, we are smarter, and we slowly realize that the watch is worth $30 or $300—both of which show the same time. Whether we carry a purse worth $30 or $300, the amount of money in the wallets are the same. Whether we drive a car worth $150,000 or a car worth $30,000, the road and distance are the same. We reach the same destination. If we drink a bottle worth $300 or wine worth $10, the

'stroller' will be the same. If the house we live in is 300 square meters or 3,000 square meters, the loneliness is the same.

Your true inner happiness does not come from the material things of this world. Whether you're flying first class or economy class, if the plane crashes, you crash with it.

So I hope you understand that when you have friends or someone to talk to, this is true happiness!

**Five Undeniable Facts**

1. Do not educate your children to be rich. Educate them to be happy, so when they grow up, they will know the value of things, not the price.
2. Eat your food as medicine. Otherwise, you will need to eat your medicine as food.
3. Whoever loves you will never leave you, even if he has one hundred reasons to give up. He will always find one reason to hold on.
4. There is a big difference between *being human* and *human being*.
5. If you want to go fast, go alone. But if you want to go far, go together.

And in conclusion . . .

**The six best doctors in the world are**

1. Sunlight
2. Rest
3. Exercise
4. Diet
5. Self-confidence
6. Friends

Keep them in all stages of life and enjoy a healthy life.

Whichever stage in life we are at right now, with time, we will face the day when the curtain comes down.

Treasure love for your family, love for your spouse, love for your friends.

Treat yourself well. Cherish others.

Beware of destination happiness. If you are not happy now, you won't be when you get there. Remember the chapter on gratitude.

Maybe the key to being happy is knowing you have the power to choose what to accept and what to let go.

Happiness is a direction, not a place. One of the barriers to happiness is to manage your expectations.

Have you noticed that happy people focus on what they have, whilst unhappy people focus on what they are missing?

**Granddad Tip: Design your own 'happy hour'.**

*Let us be grateful to the people who make us happy; they are the charming gardeners who make our souls blossom.*

I believe happiness is not about getting all you want. It's about enjoying all you have.

Do relationships have to be difficult?

# 17

# Relationships

*Much better to want the mate you do not have
than to have the mate you do not want.*
—Confucius

Although a short chapter, do not underestimate the importance of good relationships.

The dictionary defines *relationship* as the connection between two people or parties.

Never leave a true relationship for a few faults. Nobody is perfect. Nobody is correct all the time. In the end, affection is always greater than perfection. Relationships are worth fighting for, but you can't be the only one fighting. A true relationship is two imperfect people refusing to give up on each other.

We looked earlier at family and friends. They lead to good or bad relationships.

Relationships lead to love and hate, and both can be controlled. Sadly, both can hurt. You have to work on the hurt because if you don't heal what hurt you, you will bleed on the people who didn't.

Hate is often love gone wrong, so try and fix it.

*Love the people God sent you. Someday he will want them back.*

Relationships are like glass. Sometimes it's better to leave them broken than try to hurt yourself putting them back together again.

I hope you fall in love with someone who never stops choosing you, and I hope you feel at home when you look at them. But we don't choose who we fall in love with, nature does that for us. Maybe the best partner is not just eye candy. Maybe they are someone who is soul food.

Keep your standards high, but try not to be too fussy. Everybody comes with baggage. Find someone who loves you enough to help you unpack.

Try to be satisfied. Many keep looking for perfection, but the grass is only greener where you water it.

Who you spend your time with is who you become. Spend your time with people who bring out the best in you, not the stress in you. Some keep dancing with the devil and wonder why they are in hell.

Don't expect everyone to always be there for you, no matter how much you do for them. Eaten bread is soon forgotten. Expect this. You will know the people who are right for you. They will make you feel better for spending time with them. The opposite, of course, is also true.

Try and figure out who is gold and who is gold-plated. My grandmother had a great saying, 'Poo on me once, shame on you. Poo on me twice, shame on me.'

Sometimes you have to let people go. Some will leave your life. That's not the end of the story. It's the end of their part in your story. Let them go so you can grow.

Avoid negative people. They de-energise you and crush your creativity.

**Granddad Tip: Sometimes you will have to unlearn the things you learnt from wounded people.**

Surround yourself with the dreamers and the doers, the believers and the thinkers, but most of all surround yourself with those who see greatness within you, even when you don't see it yourself. Don't put the key to your happiness in somebody else's pocket.

Choose the one who makes you sparkle. When Jane was asked why she married John instead of Charles, she said, 'When I'm with Charles, I feel like I am with the most important person in the world.'

'So why marry John?' she was asked.

'Ah,' said Jane. 'When I'm with John, I feel as if I'm the most important person in the world.'

*A relationship never dies a natural death. It is murdered by ego, attitude, and ignorance.*

## The Still People

Run a mile from these.

- Still broke
- Still complaining
- Still hating
- Still losing
- Still living in the past
- Still making excuses

You don't have to look for them. They will find you.

> One block to a good relationship is the blame game.
> There's a lovely Chinese proverb that says,
> He who blames others has a long way to go on his journey.
> He who blames himself is halfway there.
> He who blames no one has arrived.

## Here are some thoughts on relationships:

> *A successful marriage requires falling in love many times, always with the same person.*
> —Mignon McLaughlin

> *Love is a game that two can play and both can win.*
> —Eva Gabor

> *To know when to go away and when to come closer is the key to any lasting relationship.*
> —Doménico Cieri Estrada

*Love doesn't make the world go around. Love
is what makes the ride worthwhile.*
—Franklin P Jones

*To get the full value of joy, you must have someone to divide it with.*
—Mark Twain

*Souls tend to go back to who feels like home.*
—N R Heart

*Love does not consist in gazing at each other but in
looking outward together in the same direction.*
—Antoine de Saint-Exupéry

*I love her, and it is the beginning of everything.*
—F. Scott Fitzgerald

*In my opinion, the best thing you can do is find someone
who loves you for exactly what you are—good mood,
bad mood, ugly, pretty, handsome, what have you.*
—J K Simmons, *Juno*

Attraction requires action. Put time into this and save yourself a lot of stress. Your relationship with yourself sets the tone for every other relationship you have. This also needs work.

*Did you drop a diamond while picking up pennies?*

Time to travel now and visit other cultures.

# 18

# Why Travel and Who You Could Meet

*To move, to breathe, to fly, to float*
*To gain all while you give,*
*To roam the roads of lands remote*
*To travel is to live.*

I believe that the best education can be found between the pages of your passport.

Our beautiful planet is rich in everything we need, spread all over it. Almost every culture has contributed something great or special to our lives. This can be found in music, literature, fashion, language, sport, education, and so on. We can reach out to many countries for inspiration, knowledge, and entertainment, and there's still so much to learn as different cultures grow or regress. Have you noticed that we all smile in the same language?

**Granddad Tip: Everyone you will ever meet knows something you don't.**

I sometimes miss my pre-Internet brain, going to museums, art galleries, and cultural events.

> *To know the road ahead, ask those coming back.*
> —Old Chinese Proverb

Great nations of the past have given way to other nations growing beyond them. Huge empires have crumbled and made way for new superpowers, and even some of them have had their day as we see other superpowers emerge. Still so much to learn.

> *To travel is to discover that everyone is wrong about other countries.*
> —Aldous Huxley

Sadly, there is still racism in this world, usually based on suspicion, fear, religion, or culture; worse still, ignorance.

Maybe God had many sons that he placed strategically around about the same time. Travelling can smash this. As you visit different cultures and respect their contribution, it's much harder to criticise from a position of respect.

I am an immigrant, a native of the UK, and have lived in three countries. This has produced great friends of many different nationalities, amazing experiences of kindness and cooperation, and some dark sides. The vast majority of my experiences have been very positive. I remember the vibrant colours of Africa, the rapid growth of the Middle East, the efficiency of Germany, how big everything is in the USA, the buzz of Asia, the music and literature of Europe, how cool they are in the Caribbean, the architecture of Russia, the mystique of India, the vastness of Mongolia, the beauty of the Netherlands, the wonder of Egypt, the passion of Mexico, the cuisine of France, the splendor of Greece—all the different languages, food, music, dance. This is a beautiful world. Make sure you enjoy the uniqueness of every culture in it.

> *I would rather own little and travel the world*
> *than own the world and travel little of it.*
> —Alexander Sattler

Please travel and learn from the best, and don't be afraid to roll your sleeves up and help where required. Many countries need help because of circumstances beyond their control. The main culprits are climate, war, and corruption; in some countries, combination of these. We will cover 'giving back' later.

*Travelling, it leaves you speechless, then turns you into a storyteller.*

*We travel not to escape life but for life not to escape us.*

Up next is health, wealth, and well-being.

# 19

# Health, Wealth, and Well-Being

*Health is like money; we never have a true
idea of what it is until we lose it.
Wealth is not about having a lot of money.
It's about having a lot of options.*

**Health**

*If you are not hungry enough to eat an apple,
you're not hungry, you're bored.*

Health is a state of complete physical, mental, and social well-being and not merely the absence of disease or infirmity.

Health is the biggest wealth for you in your entire lifetime. You can survive without a lot of money, but you can't survive without good health. Health is something that we can't buy with money, but we can take care of it, and we can cure it when needed with the help of the money. If you are not having good health, you will not be able to enjoy your life to the fullest. Money doesn't make you rich and happy but good health does. You can't feel complete and happy without good health. And if you think eating healthy is expensive, just wait 'til you see the medical bills for eating bad food.

A healthy lifestyle will bring more happiness than you can imagine.

Doctors are turning the tables on us. Modern medicine and a better lifestyle are extending our life expectancies. On the other hand, poor lifestyle is causing people to live unhealthily and reducing life expectancy. It's not just about what you eat. It's about what you think and say to yourself.

Taking care of your overall health and well-being is the healthy cherry on your cake. And it's not just about eating and exercise. It's about thinking as well.

*Eat crap and get a big fat ass for free.*

If you only had one car for the rest of your life, you'd look after it, wouldn't you? Polish it, change the oil, ensure the engine is free from dirt or clogging. That car is your body. Yet we do not always remember it's the only one we will have. What you eat in private you wear in public.

Who is the best doctor to look after this? You are your best nurse and doctor.

Have you ever thought about how wonderful your body really is? Your eyes are a great camera. Your ears filter out bad sounds. Your voice is an amazing microphone. Your bones hold you up. Your veins carry fuel around your body. Your heart is a sophisticated pump. Your liver and kidneys filter out impurities. Your immune system protects you from germs. Your brain coordinates all this.

You are truly an amazing creation with every part of your body connected and working together. Why would we try to prevent or spoil this? That's exactly what we do by not taking care of this wonderful creation.

All your body asks in return is eat well, exercise, and keep your brain active and calm. That's not so bad, is it?

Don't dig your grave with your own knife and fork. If you don't make time for your wellness, you will be forced to make time for your illness.

**Granddad Tip: Living is a contact sport, whatever your position, so might as well prepare and get in shape.**

In the chapter on happiness, I quoted Steve Jobs who had a lot to say about happiness linked to health. It's worth reminding ourselves again who he thought were our best doctors.

The six best doctors in the world:

1. Sunlight
2. Rest
3. Exercise
4. Diet
5. Self-Confidence
6. Friends

Love your body. The payback is amazing. It's been with you through it all. It's more faithful to you than anything else. It will carry you for as long as it can, and you control much of that. It lets you know when it needs rest. It lets you know when you are feeling stressed. It tries to speak to you about the beauty that you have that the world can't understand.

Many are killing themselves to live, one mouthful at a time. Bad food is only good for your mouth, not your body. If you can master your diet, you can master anything. Disciplining your food intake is the best habit you can develop. When your diet is wrong, medicine is of no use. When your diet is correct, medicine is of no need.

Medicine is not health care. Food is health care. Medicine is sick care. Think about that.

Someone once said rest. I put my heart and body into my work and lost my soul in the process. But rest is important to recharge. You cannot see your face in running water. You can only see it in still water. There is a time to do nothing and benefit from it.

Are you dying to live? No, you're living to die. The clock starts when you were born.

'Your body. It just has always, and will always, simply want to be your friend,' said S C Lourie, so let her finish this chapter on health.

*Love your body, darling.*
*It's been with you through it all.*
*It's more faithful to you than anything else.*
*It will love you unconditionally until its last breath.*
*It will carry you for as long as it can.*
*It lets you know when you need rest.*
*It lets you know when you're getting too stressed.*

*It tries to speak with you about the beauty*
*that you have that the world*
*can't understand.*
*It just has always and will always simply want to be your friend.*

## Exercise

*I hate training, but I love having trained.*

That lovely feeling when your body says thanks. When you put the right fuel in and take it for a test run.

We know we can't out-exercise a bad diet, so let's get that right first.

When you exercise, you eat healthier, you're more focussed, so you think clearer. Crisper thoughts flow easier. You sleep better. Exercise pushes you towards your best self.

Fitness is not 30 percent gym and 70 percent diet. It's 100 percent dedication to the gym when you're there and to your diet when you're not. When your body gets tired, say this: 'This is where winners are made.' How does that feel?

Many are killing themselves one mouthful at a time or improving their lives one mouthful at a time, building a new body with every bite you take.

*Training starts in the kitchen.*
—Dee Ludlow

You could start by walking 25 percent faster. That will increase your momentum, which is great exercise, and lose a load of calories as a bonus. Your body will love you for it.

When you have good health and wealth, you have good well-being. I read a good article from India written by a yoga expert, which went into depth on the advantages of Asian techniques to help with relaxation, posture, etc. I cannot remember her name, but I remember her quote: 'Are you wearing your nature well?' What does that mean to you?

*Nurture your nature.*

**Granddad Tip: You are only one workout away from a good mood.**

# Wealth

### Money – Financial Wellness

*The rich stay rich by spending like the poor. The poor stay poor by spending like the rich.'*

This comes in many guises: wealth management, financial coaching, financial advice, etc.

By the time you read this, you will be well versed with what money does. Sadly, many people have a bad relationship with money.

It can be hard to keep, but keep some you must. Money is hard to earn and easy to love. Guard yours with care.

**Create a Wealth Vision**

This is the first step. What can you imagine for the future? What do you want for the future? Do you see abundance or average? Get this right now and you will want to review this again and again as your plan grows. You know the importance of vision now. Think how exciting it will be to create the wealth you visualise.

Now make it a plan.

**Your Wealth Plan**

*This is how to up your game with money.*

So what's this plan and what should it include? This is a project for the future of your money. Let's get it right.

You are not too young to start and never forget You are the bank of your future.

The following is the agenda of a course I designed. Take a look below and see the elements of a good plan. These are the main things to consider and find out.

**Granddad Tip: Put time into your plan well in advance. It wasn't raining the day Noah built the ark.**

**Creating and Mastering Your Wealth**

*Taking control of your finances . . . from today.*

It starts with . . .

1. **Your Wealth Vision - Creating Your Financial Future**

- The importance of vision
- What do you want?
- What's in your way?
- Your vision blueprint
- Removing your obstacles
- Exercises

Next up . . .

2. **Your Foundations - Your Personal Balance Sheet**

*A snapshot of where you are now.*

- Where are you now, personally and financially?
- How to build on this?
- How do experts use a balance sheet?
- Building on *your* balance sheet

It's launch time.

3. **Creating Your Future Budget**

*A budget is telling your money where to go instead of wondering where it went.*

- The elements of a good budget
- Budgetary constraints hello
- Tips and motivation to save money
- Your income and where it could come from
- Allocating your income
- Checks and balances

- Surplus and deficits
- Cash flow
- Teach your children to save money
- Exercises

*If your outgoings exceed your income then
your upkeep is your downfall.*

Now for takeoff . . .

4. **Building Your Future Capital**

   *It's the first pound that makes the most money.*

- The importance of regular savings
- Options
- Pound-cost averaging
- Simple and compound interest
- Tax and how to reduce it
- Inflation and how to fight it
- Risk and time horizon
- Typical costs and charges
- Sample projections and illustrations of savings plans

Looking after your capital . . .

5. **Capital Investment**

- Likely sources for you
- Investment basics
- Design your first investment portfolio
- Advantages of parents transferring capital to you
- Inflation and how to fight it

- Risk and time horizon
- Getting your feet wet
- Typical costs and charges
- Sample projections and illustrations of savings plans
- Access to your capital
- Taking income
- The importance of diversification
- Your future ATM
- Investment products
- The advisors and how to deal with them

*Free advice—how much did that cost you?*

6. **Secrets of Debt Management**

*There's no greater dignity than to live within one's income.*

- Types of debt
- Secured
- Unsecured
- Credit cards – pretend money
- Debt management
- Typical costs of debt
- How do interest rates work: APR
- Your credit score and what it means
- Mortgages and secured loans

*Those who understand interest collect it. Those who don't, pay it.*

Keeping it all together for the people you love . . .

7. **Protecting Everything You Care About**

- How much is enough?
- Gap analysis
- Insurance and how to arrange it
- Insurance products: How they work and typical costs
- What affects the cost?
- Agreements and trusts

*Insurance is not usually for you. It's for others who depend on you.*

8. **Retirement Planning**

   *Will you enjoy retirement or retire from enjoyment?*

- This is what it's all about for you, when, and how
- Reverse engineer your income and capital needs
- Gap analysis
- The products and investments
- Tax and allowances

9. **Estate Planning**

   *This is what it's all about for them.*

- Who gets what and how?
- Estate calculation gross
- Estate calculation net (after inheritance tax (IHT))
- What is IHT?
- What are your allowances against IHT?
- How to use wills?
- How to use trusts?
- What is probate?
- Speeding the distribution of the proceeds of an estate

*Being rich is having money. Being wealthy is having time.*

## Well-Being

*Almost everything will work again if you unplug it for a few minutes, including you.*
—Anne Lamott

In nature, nothing exists alone. Look how beautiful everything else is connected from the plants to science. We are part of this, so ask yourself sometimes, are you wearing your nature well?

You have a communication system linked to every part of your body. Be careful what you are saying. It's just like Siri or Alexa.

It's okay to refresh, reboot, reload, and release. Your body benefits from movement, whilst your mind benefits from stillness.

We spoke earlier of a to-do list and a not-to-do list. How about a *to-be* list?

- Be healthy.
- Be awesome.
- Be calm.
- Be helpful.
- Be happy.

It starts with your body and mind. You can reinvent your body and resurrect your soul. Aim for peace, for once you get a taste of peace, you will cut anyone off to keep it.

Make yourself a priority once in a while. It's not selfish. It's necessary.

Go to the beach and listen to the waves. It's the only place salt lowers your blood pressure. The beach doesn't ask questions.

Why not become an ambassador of peace in your own life? Your life will become a masterpiece when you learn to master peace.

*Are you mindful or mind full?*

## Mental Health

If you want perfect health, then first of all, you have to improve the quality of the thoughts you generate in your mind. When you think positively, you improve the chemistry from within. For a healthy lifestyle, you could follow many rules and should also sacrifice many things in your daily routines.

It's so easy to get down and get sucked into problems, often others.

When you are inwardly confident by using the right thinking, you do not have to reach out for help. You can reach in.

**Granddad Tip: Beware of negative people. They are hard wired for misery.**

Largely down to thinking, have you ever met anyone who is forward-thinking, goal-orientated, working on it, and depressed? Have you met anyone who's depressed who is forward-thinking, goal-oriented and working on it? Think about that.

Mental health is real, and the best medicine I've found is to control it with the right thinking.

Even though there are some days you will wish you could change things from the past, there's a reason the rear-view mirror is so small and the windscreen is so big. Where you are heading is much more important than what you left behind.

## 'Thinking'
## Walter D Wintle

If you think you are beaten, you are.
If you think you dare not, you don't.
If you like to win but think you can't,
It's almost certain you won't.
If you think you'll lose, you've lost,
For out of the world, we find
Success begins with a person's will.
It's all in the state of mind.
If you think you are outclassed, you are,
You've got to think high to rise.
You've got to be sure of yourself before
You can ever win a prize.
Life's battles don't always go
To the stronger or faster man,
But sooner or later, the one that wins
Is the one who THINKS HE CAN.

*It's easier to slim than to lose weight. You're attached to the weight.*

Generally, a healthy lifestyle is the highest blessing that we should not take for granted. It is the main source of all the happiness in someone's life. Money can help you in buying all the luxuries in this world, but it cannot buy you good health. A person is totally responsible for his/her health, and he/she has to take care of his/her health in all the possible ways by avoiding a few things and by adopting some new and good habits that lead to a healthy life. So for well-being and happiness, it is important to switch to a healthy lifestyle.

If health, wealth, and well-being were intertwined or woven together, imagine what that would do for your life.

**Granddad Tip: Get addicted—addicted to personal development.**

Finally, we all are aware that our health is the most important wealth that we have. We know that we can earn money, and if we lose it, we can it get back. Not so with our health.

Whilst I'm advocating great health and looking after yourself, even people who achieve great things may be in poor health. And you never know when bad health or an accident can strike. Your body will compensate for weaknesses if you let it. There are so many examples of people who were physically challenged who achieved great success using their brains. One example is Prof Stephen Hawking. He could not walk or move unaided. He needed a machine to help him talk. Yet he became one of the greatest physicists to live. He even made it to space.

When I was in chemotherapy, I found a new sense of urgency to achieve more. Although I felt weak and sick, I became more determined and more focussed. It was in this period that I passed some tough exams, produced the biggest deal of my career, learnt to play guitar, and started to write. This book was written when I was at stage 4 cancer. I want you to know this as it carries a powerful message. I could have done all those things better and sooner, but I didn't. These achievements took longer when I was sick, but that doesn't matter. The message is, please, please, please, please . . . DON'T WAIT TO GET SICK TO GET BETTER.

Do you know that the person you are becoming will scare the pants off the old you?

*Grow through what you go through.'*

Now let's give something back.

# 20

# Giving Back

*Your greatness is not what you have. It's what you give.*

You now have some ideas on how to enhance your life. Consider enhancing others' lives. How you walk with the broken speaks louder than how you sit with the great.

When things are exceeding your expectations, you, as a decent person, will be grateful for this.

We spoke earlier of an attitude of gratitude. What better way to show how grateful you are than by giving back, giving back to a society that helped you when you needed it? There is an emotional flood you will feel when you give back to people who need it.

It could be to your favourite charities or causes, or it could be someone who you could develop or mentor. This could be with knowledge. The biggest beneficiary of training, coaching, or mentoring is often the trainer, coach, or mentor.

It could even be working in a different country to help with their issues.

Many organisations like these will welcome your support, and you will grow by the experience.

Here's a nice story to demonstrate:

**The Farmer**

A newspaper reporter interviewed a farmer who grew award-winning maize. Each year he entered his maize in the agricultural show. It was revealed that the farmer shared his seed with his neighbours.

Amazed, the reporter asked, 'How can you afford to share your best seed with your neighbours when they are entering their maize in competition with yours each year?'

The farmer smiled knowingly and explained, 'The wind picks up pollen from the ripening maize and swirls it from field to field. If my neighbours grow inferior maize, cross-pollination will steadily degrade the quality of my maize. If I am to grow good maize, I must help my neighbours grow a good crop.'

So it is with our lives. Those who want to live meaningfully and well must help enrich the lives of others. For the value of a life is measured by the lives it touches. And those who choose to be happy must help others find happiness. For the welfare of each is bound up with the welfare of all. Call it the power of collectively. Call it a principle of success. Call it a law of life. The fact remains: 'None of us truly wins until we all win.'

Know this secret as you grow older! In life, when you help the people around you to be good, you surely become the best.

*Giving is not just about making a donation.*
*It's about making a difference.*

Now let's pull it all together and dance in your future.

# 21

# This Is Tomorrow Calling

*The biggest adventure you can take is to live the life of your dreams.*
—Oprah

Right, sassy princess, it's time to pull all this together. Now go do it, babes! Your future self is watching you right now, through your memories. You are about to begin the best year of your life. Read that bit again. Thank your past for the lessons. Tell your future you are ready. Your future needs you, your past doesn't.

Your future is not in front of you, it's inside of you. This is not about finding yourself; it's about creating yourself. Your growth will get jet lag when you are good.

I want you to enjoy your youth, but don't let it destroy your future. Mix this cocktail well. Do not get too comfortable. Comfort can be the enemy of your achievements.

When it all comes together—ka ching—yes, you can get all your planets aligned in your life: relationships, business, career, health, wealth, and wellness. How would that feel? It will always need work and maintenance, but now you know how to develop the habits you need, how to create a big vision, and where to go for help. This will add years to your life and life to your years.

It starts with a thought, then a dream, then a plan, then an action, and then a follow-through. You can't change the world, but you can change, and small steps can make big changes.

It doesn't take long to change your life when you have the confidence of knowing you are making progress, those small steps, all the way.

You now know you are the architect of your future. Design it wisely.

Words like *design* and *create* excite me. They imply I'm getting something that's not there, something I will put there from nothing. That's the magic.

Magic seems to appear when you ask yourself, how much more can turn up today?

Why should you fit in when you were born to stand out? So push limits and kick ass. Do no harm, take no shit, but get shit done.

Did you know you are a millionaire? You just haven't had the money yet.

Did you know you are an author? You just haven't finished your book yet.

Did you know you are a warrior? You just haven't had your crown yet.

What else did you know?

Our success is never owned, only rented, and rent is due every day. Up to 86,400 seconds is the price. There is no secret to success. There's a system. Use the knowledge in this book to develop your own system. When your health, mind, and actions are in place, you can take on the world. Invest in your future because this is where you will spend the rest of your life.

Are you ready to take on the world? It's waiting for you. Now get your eyes on the prize. Polish your life with class, and don't let anyone turn off that smile.

The past is in your head, and your future is in your hands. You will lose friends when you get serious about your goals, but it's worth it. You need the right friends in your future. If they can't think like you, they will not fit in with your aspirations. They may not even understand why you are doing this. That's why only about 10 percent of the UK population pay higher rate tax. Many will quote tradition as an excuse not to change. They say, 'This is the way we've always done things.' Well, remind them that you are the agent of change because 'tradition was meant to be a rudder, not an anchor.'

You can say yes to so many things, but never forget the power of saying, 'No, thank you.' It's quite liberating to say no, knowing that's the end of it. Sometimes saying yes gets you firmly into others' problems and issues. Choose carefully before saying yes or no. We are increasingly defined by the things we say no to.

Watch the company you keep. We do not take swimming lessons from drowning people. Many have narrowed their circle and increased their vision.

Remember discipline. This is the difference between what you want most and what you want now.

*Don't die with dreams. Die with memories.*

Focus. Focus on results. What's more important—being right or having the right result? We can never be right all the time, but imagine if we have a good share of the right results. You have the best success tool kit sitting on your shoulders.

> When the world is on your shoulders
> And your head feels full of lead
> And your stomach churns like butter
> And the voice inside your head
> Is reminding you of everything
> You've ever said or done,
>
> All your failures and regrets,
> And the times your fear has won,
> Take a minute to remember
> That you've survived all this before.
> You've battled and you've conquered
> When you thought you had no more.
> You are stronger than you realise.
> You are brave and wise and kind.
> And you know you're so much bigger
> Than the doubts that fill your mind.
> So breathe it in and let it out,
> Allow the ebb and flow.
> You can win this war, you always do.
> You're a warrior, you know.

The best leaders treat uncertainty as job security. They know they will come through it and emerge stronger. Those who don't will end up working for them. They know difficult roads lead to beautiful destinations, and they are not afraid to take the difficult roads.

Reinvent yourself if necessary. You can reinvent yourself as often as you like. Madonna and Bowie did it all the time. What impressed me about them is that they did it at the top of their game. They would create a new image or character and change it when it was successful. That's a big risk, but when you are at the top of your game, you can take more risks. If you win, you will be happy. If you lose, you will be wise. So take the risk.

No matter what your past has been, you have a spotless future. I drew a line in the sand so many times that I thought I had my own beach in my head.

You will have the stories and the glories because you will learn from the past, then get the hell out of there.

Don't let the world change your smile, but allow your smile to change the world.

Seek to be well knowing rather than well-known.

You can live happily ever after, but the only way is one day at a time, and time is non-refundable, so use it wisely.

One of the secrets of being ready when everyone is watching is to work hard when no one is watching.

No matter how you feel, get up, dress up, show up, but never give up, and don't take it all too seriously because none of us are getting out of this alive.

Don't just slay your demons, dissect them and find out what they are feeding on. Then starve them.

Manage your expectations. Nothing ends nicely. That's why it ends.

*The successful warrior is like the average man with laser-like focus.*
—Bruce Lee

Make great choices.

> Choose to live by choice, not chance;
> To make changes, not excuses;
> To be motivated, not manipulated;
> To be useful, not used;
> To excel, not compete.
> Choose self-esteem, not self-pity;

To listen to your inner voice, not the random opinion of others.

Today was your tomorrow. It's up to you to shape it, to take control, and to seize those opportunities. The power is in the choices you make every day. Eat well, sleep well, think well. You shape you. You won't find the will power; you have to create it. The reality is it's you against you.

Boss this chapter. When you own the story, you can write the ending and leave a little sparkle wherever you go.

Relax and be you, the real you. You don't need to impress anyone. Tension is who you are trying to be. Peace is who you are. This is where well-being kicks in.

We spoke of stepping stones earlier, there are stumbling blocks too, but the difference is how you use them.

One of the biggest movie franchises of my day was a boxing hero called Rocky, always the underdog and came back from ridiculous odds. Although a bit far-fetched, it made great entertainment and was very inspirational. Here's his lecture to his son when he tried to motivate him:

> *The world ain't all sunshine and rainbows. It's a very mean and nasty place. And I don't care how tough you are. It will beat you to your knees and keep you there permanently if you let it. You, me, or nobody is gonna hit as hard as life. But it ain't about how hard you hit. It's about hard you can get hit and keep moving forward. How much can you take and keep moving forward? That's how winning is done.*
> *—Rocky Balboa*

Go shuffle and shift and let the sparks of possibility become the flames of your future. Everything is on loan. When a bird is alive, it eats ants. When it's dead, they eat him.

We all know what giving up feels like. Go and show them what happens when you don't.

> *Have no fear of perfection. You will never reach it.*
> *—Salvador Dali*

Put energy into whatever makes your heart sing and deal with the stress. An arrow can only be launched by pulling it backwards, so when life is pulling you back with difficulties, maybe it's about to launch you into something great. You can't change anything from your past, but you can change everything in your future.

Now get out there and serve up all your value. Shine your light on everyone. Respect the power of words. Choose them carefully. They can build and destroy.

Go after the gains and aggregate them however small. Baby successes create a great future.

I once heard that you can take a horse to water, but you can't make him drink. The same people believe you can't teach an old dog new tricks. This is not true. You can raise the water lip high and make waves. He'll soon drink. And many an old dog learnt new tricks when they were open-minded.

It's your world now. Look after it. It's your future now. Keep creating it. Your soul is screaming for this. Now enjoy it.

Your world will be very different from mine. You are living in the most exciting time in history. World knowledge is doubling every twelve months, and that figure is reducing. The silicon chip doubles in capacity every eighteen months, leading to amazing scientific breakthroughs. It's called Moore's law. That too is reducing.

I'm pretty sure that . . .

- Drones will deliver most things.
- There will be no cash.

- Cars will fly and not require a driver.
- Schools will be in the cloud.
- Shopping done from your watch.
- Interplanetary travel will be the norm.
- Robots will clean and cook for you.

Keep checking on your goals. Are they on track, in danger, or need attention?

Why not consider a letter from your future self? What would it include? Where will you be when you write it? How healthy will you be? How does it feel? Is it nice to have lots of security, including financial?

It would be my great pleasure if you passed this down to your grandchildren and involve your children in the process.

> *You always had the power, my dear. You just had to learn it for yourself.*
> —Glinda, the witch in the *Wizard of Oz*

A flower doesn't think of competing. It just blooms. When everything is in place, just watch how you will bloom. Bloom into the best possible version of you. Then you could have a life to remember or one they will never forget. Learn to trust yourself. Some of the best advice you will get will come from your instincts.

Imagine the majesty of sitting on the throne of your own world. You don't need royal blood if you include in your life

- Big dreams and vision
- Personal goals in place and monitored
- Attitude and belief in your ability

- Great habits
- Laser focus
- No procrastination
- Taking massive action
- Total commitment
- A dropped ego
- Focussing on learning and education
- Staying close to your family and friends
- Travelling and learning from different cultures
- Giving back
- Listen to tomorrow calling

Let these flow through your veins, and your imagination will come to you, with all the things you want, and do it yourself. You are the artist of your future. Don't give your paintbrush to someone else.

I am quite old at the time of writing, so I may not be here when you are ready to read this. If that's the case, I will leave the light on in heaven for you, and you can read your book to your grandchildren.

And finally, don't be frightened to love yourself. You do not need to be a philosopher, a professor, or religious leader to write great inspirational verse. Here is an unexpected philosopher, the late great Whitney Houston from her song 'The Greatest Love of All.' Let's let her finish this.

> I believe the children are our are future.
> Teach them well and let them lead the way.
> Show them all the beauty they possess inside.
> Give them a sense of pride to make it easier.
> Let the children's laughter remind us how we used to be.
> Everybody's searching for a hero.

People need someone to look up to.
I never found anyone who fulfilled my needs,
A lonely place to be,
And so I learned to depend on me.
I decided long ago
Never to walk in anyone's shadows.
If I fail, if I succeed,
At least I'll live as I believe.
No matter what they take from me,
They can't take away my dignity
Because the greatest
Love of all is happening to me.
I found the greatest
Love of all inside of me.
The greatest love of all
Is easy to achieve.
Learning to love yourself,
It is the greatest love of all.

*It's your time now. Go hustle, babes. Make it worth it.*

With love from Gandad Honky Konky, a dreamer, a drifter, a storyteller, and a very proud granddad

# Suggested Further Reading

### Great Books for Teens

Christen, Carol. *What Color Is Your Parachute.*

Covey, Dsean. *The Six Most Important Decisions You'll Ever Make.*

Cranfield, Jack. *The Success Principles for Teens.*

Harris, Alex and Brett. *Do Hard Things.*

McClutcheon, Megan. *The Ultimate Self-Esteem Workbook for Teens.*

Peale, Norman Vincent. *The Power of Positive Thinking.*

Saul, Aunt Laya. *You Don't Have to Learn Everything the Hard Way.*

Smile Press. *Do Your Best, Forget the Rest.*

# Thanks and Acknowledgements

I am grateful to the following for the help, support, inspiration, and love:

- The wonderful medical teams in the United Kingdom and Hong Kong, in particular Neville Hall Hospital, Abergavenny and Queen Mary Hospital, Hong Kong. Without you, I would not be here.
- My close friends who always understood and were there for me, especially during chemo: Moose Martin, Tecky Tillery, Baggins Conner, Cristal (Chica) Vazquez, the communities in Mui Wo and South Wales.
- St James's Place, the most compassionate employer possible and amazing work colleagues.
- My clients all over the world from thirty-seven years in this wonderful business, too many to mention.

- Jason Pearce and Elaine Gately for humbling me with their editing skills.
- Mini for her unconditional love and support over the last three years.
- Theresa Ludlow, the best sister any brother could wish for.
- My pack: Lidia and Shara for looking after and supporting my sons, my ex-wife Michelle whose concern was much appreciated.
- My sons Daniel and Jack who turned the tables on me and became my inspiration, my mentors, and my best buddies.
- And to the true inspiration for this book, Skylah, Chanel, and Tienna.

Printed in Great Britain
by Amazon